NFL 100

THE GREATEST MOMENTS OF
THE NFL'S CENTURY

CRAIG ELLENPORT

30 YEARS

TRIUMPH
BOOKS

Triumph Books LLC
814 North Franklin Street
Chicago, Illinois 60610
(312) 337-0747
www.triumphbooks.com

Printed in U.S.A.
ISBN: 978-1-62937-745-2
Design by Jonathan Hahn

TO MY OWN HALL OF FAMERS:
MY WIFE, RANDI, AND MY TWO BOYS, SAM AND BEN.

CONTENTS

Foreword *by Troy Aikman*   IX

Introduction   XI

1 The Greatest Game Ever Played   1

2 The Guarantee   3

3 The Merger   4

4 Birth of NFL Films   6

5 Perfection   8

6 Ice Bowl   11

7 Debut of *Monday Night Football*   12

8 The Catch   14

9 Breaking the Color Barrier   17

10 Red Grange's Pro Debut, Barnstorming
Tour   18

11 Rozelle Becomes Commissioner   21

12 Super Bowl LI: The Comeback   22

13 Super Bowl I   24

14 Bears Win 1940 Title, 73–0   26

15 Lombardi Named Packers Coach   28

16 Chiefs Win Super Bowl IV   33

17 Dawn of America's Team   35

18 Jim Brown's Hall of Fame Career Comes to
an End   36

19 Super Bowl XXV: Wide Right   39

20 Almost-Perfect Patriots   40

21 Immaculate Reception   43

22 NFL-AAFC Merger   45

23 Joe Montana's Super Bowl XXIII Magic   47

24 First NFL Draft   48

25 NFL's Leadership after 9/11   50

26 Walter Payton Passes Jim Brown   53

27 Shula Wins No. 325   54

28 Patriots Dynasty Born   56

29 First Nationally Televised Title Game   59

30 First Championship Game   62

31 Congress Okays Single-Network TV Deals   64

32 Otto Graham's Last Game . . . and Seventh
Title   67

33 Pro Football Hall of Fame Opens   68

34 AFL's Challenge   70

35 Birth of the Pittsburgh Steelers Dynasty   72

36 New Rules to Create More Offense   74

37 Miracle at the Meadowlands   76

38 NFL Draft on ESPN   78

39 Epic in Miami: Chargers-Dolphins Playoff
Game   81

40 Slingin' Sammy's "Triple Crown"   82

41 Halas' Last Title   84

42 Riggo's Super Bowl Heroics   87

43 Sneakers Game   88

44 Six TDs for Sayers   92

45 Greatest Draft Ever   94

46 Four Straight Super Bowls for Bills   97

47 Super Bowl Halftime Becomes a Spectacle   98

48 Tagliabue Named Commissioner   100

49 The *Heidi* Game   103

50 O.J. Tops 2,000   105

51 Crazylegs Smashes Receiving Record   111

52 Sea of Hands   113

53	The Drive	114
54	Bell Named Commissioner	116
55	First TV Megadeal	118
56	The Comeback: Bills-Oilers	122
57	1998 NFL Draft: Manning or Leaf	124
58	Dan Marino's Record-Breaking Season	127
59	Free Substitution Allowed	128
60	Chiefs-Dolphins' Double OT	130
61	"Super Bowl Shuffle"	132
62	New CBA Opens Door for Modern-Day Free Agency	134
63	Eric Dickerson's Record-Breaking Season	137
64	Jerry Rice's Record-Breaking Season	139
65	"This One's for John"	140
66	Barry Sanders Retires	143
67	Super Bowl XXXIV: One Yard Short	144
68	NFL vs. USFL	146
69	Super Bowl XXII: Doug Williams	150
70	Raiders vs. the NFL	153
71	Philly Special	154
72	Pete Gogolak Poached by Giants	157
73	Colts Leave Baltimore	158
74	Reggie White Signs with Packers	160
75	Emmitt Is New Rushing King	163
76	NFL Approves Names on Jerseys	164
77	Brees Breaks Passing Record	166
78	Super Bowl XIII: The Rematch	168
79	Music City Miracle	170
80	Adoption of Rooney Rule	172
81	Birth of NFL Network	175
82	Super Bowl XLIII: The Catch	176
83	DirecTV Launches NFL Sunday Ticket	178
84	Saints Return to New Orleans . . . and Stay There	181
85	Favre Honors Dad	183
86	Peyton Rides into Sunset	185
87	Bill Belichick Named Patriots Head Coach	186
88	Goodell Named Commissioner	189
89	NFL Adopts Instant Replay	190
90	FOX Lands NFL Rights	194
91	Michael Strahan Breaks Sack Record, with Help	196
92	APFA Becomes NFL; Decatur Staleys Become Chicago Bears	199
93	Rams-Colts Franchise Trade	200
94	The Fumble	203
95	Roger Staubach and the NFL's First Hail Mary	204
96	Joe Carr Named President of APFA	207
97	Derrick Thomas Sets Single-Game Sack Record	210
98	Cleveland Loses, Keeps Browns	212
99	Adrian Peterson's Single-Game Rushing Record	215
100	RedZone Channel Launch	217
	Acknowledgments	220
	Photo Attribution	221
	About the Author	223

FOREWORD

The first regular-season NFL game I ever attended as a fan may not qualify as one of the greatest moments in the first 100 years of the league's history, but it's not an exaggeration to say it had a profound impact on my life.

It was during my senior year at UCLA. I was visiting a friend in Phoenix and the Cardinals were hosting the Green Bay Packers in the last game of the 1988 season, so we went. It really was a coincidence that I was there. The Packers entered that day tied with the Dallas Cowboys for the worst record in the league, and the Packers had already told me they were going to take me if they got the first pick in the 1989 Draft. Dallas lost to Philadelphia earlier that day. If the Packers lost, Green Bay would clinch the No. 1 pick. If they won, Dallas would get the pick.

Full disclosure: I was rooting for the Packers to win.

Not that I had anything against Green Bay, I just didn't want to play in the cold. I struggled throwing a wet ball, and I just thought Green Bay would be a tough fit for me. Plus, I was 12 years old when my family moved from California to Oklahoma—and that was Cowboys country. So the thought of getting to play for the team that was only a few hours from my hometown was very appealing.

Like I said, it won't be recognized as one of the greatest games in NFL history, but it was significant to me. The Packers actually trailed late in the first half, until Green Bay quarterback Don Majkowski threw a pair of touchdown passes to seal the win—which is ultimately how I became a Cowboy.

Thank you, Majik Man.

That's one of the funny things about the NFL. You don't always know what you're going to get.

I mentioned that was the first regular-season NFL game I had ever seen in person. About 10 months before that, I was actually at Super Bowl XXII at Jack Murphy Stadium in San Diego.

The owner of the event staff that worked the game was a UCLA alum, so me and a bunch of UCLA players went down to work the game—got paid $20. When the game began, I found a perch in the stadium where I could just watch the game. So I "worked" that game—but watched it more than anything.

As far as history goes, the Denver Broncos jumped out to a 10–0 lead and it looked for sure like I was about to witness John Elway win his first Super Bowl. But that narrative changed completely in the second quarter, as the Washington Redskins came storming back. When it was over, I had seen something even more historic: the Redskins' Doug Williams, who was the game's MVP, became the first African American starting quarterback to win the Super Bowl.

The NFL is rich with history. As a child of the '70s, my mind goes back to the iconic teams of that decade: the Oakland Raiders, with John Madden roaming the sidelines and Kenny Stabler at quarterback . . . Fran Tarkenton and the Vikings . . . the Pittsburgh Steelers dynasty that won four Super Bowls in six years.

Pittsburgh's fourth title during that stretch was won against the Rams. I was a big Rams fan growing up, watching quarterbacks James Harris and Pat Haden.

Then Vince Ferragamo took them to the Super Bowl. I can still name so many of the starters from that team, on both sides of the ball: Jack Youngblood . . . Jim Youngblood . . . Lawrence McCutcheon . . . Wendell Tyler . . . Jackie Slater . . . Nolan Cromwell . . . Fred Dryer.

That was my exposure to the NFL at a young age, and I've been a fan of the league ever since. It was a dream come true for me to make it to that level, and then I was blessed to be a part of three Super Bowl championship teams with the Dallas Cowboys. Making it to the Pro Football Hall of Fame is an honor that still blows me away. I have to pinch myself sometimes and wonder if I belong in there. But being in the Hall has given me the chance to get to know Jack Youngblood, one of my favorites as a fan growing up, and he is everything that I hoped he would be.

The same holds true for Roger Staubach, who I've gotten to know well, of course, through the Cowboy connection. We've been friends, we've been business partners, and he's been a mentor in some ways, too.

It's good to know that these people, when you meet them, are all men of high character. That can be said for so many of the people that have shaped the first 100 years of the National Football League.

It's been a real privilege for me to have been a fan as a kid, then play the game and hopefully contribute to that history, and now to be a part of it on the other side as a broadcaster.

Television has been such a vital part of the NFL's history. Staying up late to watch *Monday Night Football* was such a big deal when I was a kid. I remember watching Tony Dorsett's 99-yard run when it happened. I was a sophomore at the University of Oklahoma when I watched in real time as Joe Theismann broke his leg. The *Monday Night Football* trio of Don Meredith, Frank Gifford, and Howard Cosell was the standard that other broadcast teams were measured against. Then came Madden and Pat Summerall, and those two presented us some of the most memorable moments in NFL history as well.

As a broadcaster myself, I'm thrilled to have the opportunity to watch a lot of these moments that people will be talking about 100 years from now.

I had the good fortune to be in the broadcast booth for FOX Sports when David Tyree made the "helmet catch" that helped the New York Giants shock the unbeaten New England Patriots in Super Bowl XLII. I was there nine years later when the Patriots made their unbelievable comeback from a 28–3 deficit to defeat the Atlanta Falcons in overtime of Super Bowl LI.

We all knew those were historic games. Everyone around the world thought that. Outside of actually playing in those games, to be a part of them as a broadcaster is about as good as it gets.

Then again, anyone who watches these moments—in the stadium or on television—knows the feeling. We all get that same rush of adrenaline, burst of excitement, and even a wave of emotion when we witness them.

It's been that way in the NFL for 100 years. And it's not about to change anytime soon.

—**Troy Aikman**
May 2019

INTRODUCTION

I t only seems as if the National Football League has been conducting business from high-powered offices in big buildings on New York City's Park Avenue for the last 100 years. In fact, the league was based in suburban Philadelphia back in the '50s, and Chicago before that.

Of course, the first formal meeting of pro football team owners took place in a much more humble setting: an automobile showroom in downtown Canton, Ohio.

The showroom belonged to Ralph Hay, a car dealer who also happened to own the Canton Bulldogs (seen playing below). Hay called the meeting, which took place on August 20, 1920, between the owners of the four professional football teams from the state of Ohio: the Bulldogs, Akron Pros, Cleveland Indians, and Dayton Triangles. The result of that meeting was the formation

of the American Professional Football Conference, which would become the National Football League.

Less than a month later, on September 17, a second meeting was held. In addition to the four Ohio teams, representatives of others from nearby states were there: the Hammond Pros and Muncie Flyers from Indiana; the Rochester Jeffersons from New York; and the Rock Island Independents, Racine Cardinals, and Decatur Staleys from Illinois. There weren't enough seats in Hay's Hupmobile showroom to go around, so many in attendance had to sit along the running boards of the Hupmobiles. One of the car-sitters was none other than George Halas, owner of the Decatur Staleys—soon to change their name to the Chicago Bears.

Can you imagine Jerry Jones sitting on a running board in an auto showroom while conducting NFL

business? And it's fair to say that Jones has never been involved in a league meeting as important as the one that took place on that day in Canton.

It's not that professional football didn't exist before then. But leagues that were formed were strictly regional, limited to teams within the same state. There were no regulations in place and players jumped from team to team—wherever they could get the most money.

At that September 17 meeting, the American Professional Football Conference became the American Professional Football Association. Jim Thorpe, who joined the Canton Bulldogs in 1915 after winning gold at the 1912 Olympics, was named president of the APFA.

The rest, as they say, is history.

So where do those pivotal meetings—which led to the birth of the most successful sports league in American history—rank among the most important moments in NFL history?

As we celebrate the 100th anniversary of these historic meetings, it doesn't seem fair to place them in the mix of the most significant events that were to follow. They stand on their own; without them, there would be no iconic NFL games, no mythic players, no legendary moments that changed the way we watch and think of professional sports.

Those organizational meetings set the stage for a decade of fits and starts. That inaugural 1920 season featured 14 teams, only two of which—the Staleys (soon to be Bears) and Cardinals—are still around today. A year later, there were 21 teams.

Think about it. In today's NFL, the birth of one new franchise—or the shuttering of a franchise—would be major news. In the first 16 years of the NFL, there was never a string of consecutive seasons with the same roster of teams. Check out the breakdown of the number of teams in the NFL those seasons:

1920	14
1921	21
1922	18
1923	20
1924	18
1925	20
1926	22

The Green Bay Packers try to bring down Benjamin Friedman of the New York Giants during a November 1929 game at the Polo Grounds.

1927	12
1928	10
1929	12
1930	11
1931	10
1932	8
1933	10
1934	11
1935	9

The pivotal year was 1927. At a special meeting, league president Joe Carr decided to consolidate. Weeding out the financially weaker teams, the NFL shrunk from 22 teams to 12. With the better players from the disbanded teams joining with the 12 remaining teams, the talent level immediately rose. The New York Giants—who nearly folded after their inaugural 1925 season but were saved when a visit from superstar Red Grange stirred fan interest—posted 10 shutouts in 13 games and won the championship that year.

As turbulent as these early years were, there were several seminal moments that occurred—some of which did indeed make this list.

What you'll find in this book is a rundown of the top 100 most . . . well, what exactly is the most appropriate term? Important? Iconic? Memorable? Unforgettable? Game-changing? Let's say, these are the greatest and most influential moments in the history of an organization that is rich with history.

Some are significant off-the-field changes and business decisions that had a profound effect on the game. Some are record-breaking performances or games that have earned a storied status in the annals of the sport. Some are simply start or end dates for the careers of players and coaches without whom the game's history could not be written.

Will you agree with the exact order of this list? Highly doubtful. Are there moments you think are missing? Highly probable.

Let's see.

1

THE GREATEST GAME EVER PLAYED

DECEMBER 28, 1958

It wasn't until 1955 that a major broadcast network, NBC to be specific, featured an NFL championship game on national television. Three years later, as the television audience grew and popularity of the sport began to take hold, the 1958 NFL Championship Game between the New York Giants and Baltimore Colts created a frenzy that elevated the sport to new heights.

Forty-five million people watched the game, the largest TV audience to that point for an NFL contest. There's a good chance that millions of those fans were watching a football game for the first time, but even those well-versed in the sport witnessed something on that day they had never seen before:

Sudden-death overtime. The first overtime playoff game in NFL history.

In order to get to overtime, legendary Colts quarterback Johnny Unitas (and this game is one of the main reasons he is legendary) engineered what is considered to be the drive that originated the term "two-minute drill." With just under two minutes to play and the Colts trailing 17–14, Baltimore began the drive on their 14-yard line. On third-and-10, Unitas found Hall of Fame running back Lenny Moore for 11 yards. After an incompletion, he connected with Hall of Fame receiver Raymond Berry on three straight plays, putting the Colts at the Giants' 13. With seven seconds left, Steve Myhra kicked the field goal that sent the game into overtime.

Fans weren't the only ones confused. The players didn't know what to do when regulation ended. An exhibition game three years earlier had played an overtime period, but this was a first for the regular season or playoffs.

Colts head coach Weeb Ewbank told *Pro! Magazine* in 1973 that the overtime aspect of the game was really what got everyone involved so worked up. "I've never been exposed to anything like that before," he said. "It was a new experience for all of us. I tried to tell everyone just not to make any mistakes."

The Giants won the coin toss and got the ball first, but were forced to punt. Baltimore took over at their own 20 and Unitas picked up right where he left off at the end of regulation, methodically driving the Colts downfield.

They were already in field goal range when Unitas came over to Ewbank during a timeout. Ewbank told his quarterback to keep it on the ground with Alan Ameche (seen here being carried off the field), who was a reliable ballcarrier.

"Two plays later, I look up and John is throwing a pass to Jim Mutscheller," recalled Ewbank. "My heart skipped a beat, but he completed the pass and Ameche scored on the next play."

The Colts were NFL champions. Unitas had thrown for 349 yards and one touchdown. Berry caught 12 passes—an NFL playoff record that stood for decades—for 187 yards and a score. Moore had 124 yards from scrimmage.

In addition to cementing the legacy of that great Colts team, the '58 title game was the beginning of a golden age of pro football. Not only did it stimulate a fan base and trigger television's hunger for the sport, it inspired a handful of entrepreneurs who wished they could own an NFL team to start a new league: the American Football League.

2 THE GUARANTEE

JANUARY 12, 1969

In the first Super Bowl recognized at the time as "the Super Bowl," the New York Jets stunned the Baltimore Colts, 16–7, in Super Bowl III. Jets quarterback Joe Namath famously guaranteed the win and was named MVP. To this day, it remains the ultimate symbol of bold sports predictions. More importantly, in becoming the first AFL team to win the Super Bowl, the Jets' victory legitimized the upstart league and showed the world that the AFL's best could compete with the NFL's best.

Namath wasn't the only one who was confident the Jets could win. Jets head coach Weeb Ewbank—who had coached the Colts to victory in the "Greatest Game Ever Played" 10 years earlier—told *Pro! Magazine* in 1973 that it was film study in preparation for the game that led him to believe the Jets could win.

"The more we looked, the more convinced we became that we could do it," Ewbank said. "A big part was convincing our players, of course. After all, we were playing the big, bad National Football League and a Colts team that had won 15 of 16 games that season."

With the Packers winning the first two Super Bowls, NFL backers were feeling pretty good about their superiority over the AFL. Few people gave the Jets a chance to reverse the trend. The Colts were installed as 18-point favorites.

Namath didn't put up great numbers on his way to being named the MVP. He completed 17 of 28 passes for 206 yards. But he called a brilliant game, keeping the Colts defense off balance throughout. The second offensive play of the game for New York was supposed to be an off tackle to the left. Namath audibled and had Matt Snell run to the right, and Snell gained nine yards and a first down, his best run of the day. Namath knew the Colts would be double-teaming All-Pro receiver Don Maynard, which would leave George Sauer covered one-on-one. Maynard had no catches in Super Bowl III . . . but Namath found Sauer eight times for 133 yards.

The Jets have not been back to the Super Bowl since then, but their victory in Super Bowl III will forever be one of the most important contributions to the history of professional football.

"It changed the perception about the American Football League and the merger," said former Dallas Cowboys executive Gil Brandt. "That game was about the impact it had."

3 THE MERGER

JUNE 8, 1966

The National Football League was king when it came to pro football through the first 40 years of its existence, and the '60s saw the sport really blossom. But when the American Football League was formed in 1960, the NFL faced its greatest challenge. This upstart league was playing a more wide-open brand of offense. As football became a popular offering on television, the AFL provided an exciting alternative to the NFL. The two leagues began competing for top college talent.

By the middle of the decade, the AFL was gaining momentum. The NFL thought it sealed the AFL's fate when it got a lucrative two-year TV package from CBS to broadcast the 1963 and '64 seasons. But the AFL countered by signing a megadeal of its own with NBC. Competition between the leagues to sign the top players out of college started getting out of hand, but the real nastiness began when the leagues started going after established players on the other side.

as Cowboys president
Schramm

AFL commissioner
Milt Woodward

Kansas City Chiefs president
Lamar Hunt

That's when the secret meetings began. It started with meetings between Kansas City Chiefs owner Lamar Hunt and Dallas Cowboys general manager Tex Schramm.

"Very few people knew about it," said Gil Brandt, who was Schramm's second-in-command with the Cowboys. "I think the commissioner knew about it. I think [Buffalo Bills owner] Ralph Wilson, Lamar Hunt, and Tex knew about it. I'm not sure if there were any other NFL owners that knew what was going on."

NFL commissioner Pete Rozelle then came in and negotiated the deal, which would begin with an AFL-NFL World Championship Game in January 1967 and then a combined draft in 1967. Official regular-season play as one league would begin in 1970.

In addition to ending the war between the two leagues, the merger expanded the NFL from 16 teams to 26, adding major markets like Houston, Boston, and Denver. And it gave rise to the Super Bowl Era.

4 BIRTH OF NFL FILMS

APRIL 1965

"I really believe that the reason pro football shot past baseball and all the other sports by the end of the '60s, into the '70s and beyond, was because of NFL Films," said longtime sportswriter Ray Didinger, who worked at NFL Films for 13 years. "It wasn't the sole reason, but I think it was a big part of the reason.

"I just think NFL Films gave pro football a storytelling vehicle that no other sport had."

NFL Films, as big as it is today, came from humble roots. Ed Sabol was a topcoat salesman who tinkered with a video camera in his spare time. He would film his son Steve's high school football games, and thought enough of his work that he was inspired to launch his own film company, Blair Motion Pictures. For his first major investment, he paid the NFL $5,000 for the rights to film the 1962 NFL Championship Game.

Commissioner Pete Rozelle was so impressed with Sabol's work that he eventually negotiated an agreement for the league to purchase Blair Motion Pictures, which was renamed NFL Films. Sabol had a unique vision. This was about more than highlight reels. NFL Films combined brilliant photography, compelling narrative writing, and music to tell stories.

"Ed Sabol's idea for when he created NFL Films was that he wanted to show pro football the way Hollywood would," said Didinger. "He wanted to make a movie. And he felt the nature of the game, the way the game was played, everything about it lent itself to that. And he was right."

What NFL Films did—and continues to do—was mythologize pro football. When they chronicled the historic moments in NFL history—many of them here in this book—it was NFL Films that gave a name to these moments: the Immaculate Reception . . . The Catch . . . Sea of Hands. "All that stuff that becomes the shorthand of football history was largely provided by NFL Films," said Didinger.

Another staple of NFL Films is its regular practice of having players and coaches wear microphones on the field. To this day, the best example of that is what they got from Kansas City Chiefs head coach Hank Stram in Super Bowl IV.

"Just keep matriculating the ball down the field, boys!"

Stram was the first coach to be wired for a Super Bowl—a bold move for NFL Films considering the Minnesota Vikings were the heavy favorites in that game. Stram's colorful voice only added to NFL Films' retelling of what was one of the biggest upsets in Super Bowl history.

By then, NFL Films was well on its way, but it did take a while for some of the old-school owners of the NFL to buy into what NFL Films meant to the league in its infancy. Bears owner George Halas was one of the early doubters. He and his staff would shoo NFL Films cameramen away from the Chicago sidelines before games. They didn't believe these cameras belonged down on the field.

In time, however, Halas came to realize that Films played an important role in preserving the history of the league. He wrote a letter to Ed Sabol in which he confessed that he was wrong about NFL Films. "In my eyes," Halas wrote, "you're the keepers of the flame."

To this day, there's a banner hanging in the archives of NFL Films headquarters in New Jersey that bears Halas' words: Keepers of the Flame.

"I always thought of NFL Films as the 33rd franchise," says Didinger. "The only difference is they've never had a losing season."

5 PERFECTION

JANUARY 14, 1973

On January 14, 1973, the Miami Dolphins defeated the Washington Redskins, 14–7, to cap the NFL's first and only perfect season.

"In the annals of football history, they still don't get their due," says longtime sportswriter and NFL Films producer Ray Didinger. "When people talk about the great teams of all time, they never talk about that team. And they're the only team that went undefeated for an entire season."

The formula for success in the NFL at the time was running the football and playing defense. The '72 Dolphins had the blueprint. Don Shula's squad featured the league's top-ranked defense and the first offense in NFL history to feature a pair of 1,000-yard rushers. Led by Larry Csonka (1,117 yards) and Mercury Morris (1,000 yards), Miami broke the single-season team rushing record that had stood for 36 years. The "No-Name Defense," meanwhile, recorded three shutouts and held 11 of its 14 regular-season opponents to 17 points or less.

"I don't think there's been an offensive line that ever played as good as that offensive line did," said Didinger. "And the defense was really good. Nobody remembers any players, but they played great team defense. They never made a mistake, they never blew a coverage, never missed a tackle. They were the definition of a perfectly coached, well-disciplined team. And it didn't matter who

they were playing from week to week, they just went out and took 'em apart. It's a shame, because they don't get their due, and the further away you get from that year, the more they recede into the past.

"My god, they were a good team."

After going 14–0 during the season and then defeating Cleveland and Pittsburgh in the playoffs, Miami faced the Washington Redskins in Super Bowl VII. The Dolphins led 14–0 at halftime. Washington could do nothing against Miami's defense. The score was still 14–0 with just over two minutes left in the game when Miami lined up for a field goal attempt. How perfect . . . the Dolphins would cap a 17–0 season with a 17–0 win in the Super Bowl! What happened instead turned out to be one of the most popular bloopers in NFL history.

Garo Yepremian's kick was blocked. And the ball bounced back to Yepremian's right. The 5-foot-7 Yepremian should have fallen on the ball, but instead he picked it up, scrambled backwards, and tried to pass it. The ball went straight up in the air and it came down into the hands of Redskins cornerback Mike Bass, who ran it back 49 yards for a touchdown.

The Redskins had one last possession in the game but never really threatened. The perfect season was complete . . . even if Yepremian's blooper took a little of the bloom off it.

"Honestly, when people do a Super Bowl compilation reel now, the only play they show from that game is Garo's field goal," said Didinger. "You don't think that bugs those guys to this day? You bet it does."

6 ICE BOWL

DECEMBER 31, 1967

In the 1967 NFL Championship Game, the Green Packers defeated the Dallas Cowboys, 21–17, but the real story was the 13-below weather at Green Bay's Lambeau Field. The wind chill made it feel like minus-38. To make matters worse, the stadium's underground heating system had malfunctioned. At kickoff time, the field was a sheet of ice. Thus, Lambeau Field's timeless nickname . . . the frozen tundra.

"If they knew on Saturday that the weather would have been that cold, I don't think [NFL commissioner Pete] Rozelle would have let the game be played," said Gil Brandt, the Cowboys VP of player personnel from 1960 to 1989.

Not to take away from two outstanding defenses, but neither offense could get much going on the icy turf. Early in the fourth quarter, Dallas grabbed a 17–14 lead when running back Dan Reeves threw a halfback option pass and hit Lance Rentzel for a 50-yard touchdown. On Green Bay's last-chance drive, quarterback Bart Starr drove the Packers to the 1-yard line. On third-and-goal

from the 1, with 16 seconds left and no timeouts, Starr called his own number and followed a block from fellow Hall of Famer Jerry Kramer into the end zone for the winning score.

The defending NFL champs advanced to Super Bowl II, where they defeated the Oakland Raiders, 33–14. Starr was Super Bowl MVP for the second straight year.

Super Bowl II marked Green Bay's fifth league championship in seven years and the final title for Lombardi's Packers. None of those five title games was decided by less than nine points, so the Ice Bowl was the only real classic contest during this dynasty. Combined with the conditions, it is why this game has come to define the Packers of the '60s.

The Dallas Cowboys were clearly a team on the rise—destined to be one of the NFL's best teams of the 1970s—and the Packers were able to hold them off on this frigid day.

Thirty-two days after the Ice Bowl, Lombardi stepped down as coach of the Packers.

7 DEBUT OF *MONDAY NIGHT FOOTBALL*

SEPTEMBER 21, 1970

It was then-commissioner Pete Rozelle who had been toying with the idea of having a weekly game televised in prime time to a national audience. Legendary sports television executive Roone Arledge, who also pioneered ABC's *Wide World of Sports*, created the vehicle for Rozelle's vision. When the Cleveland Browns defeated the New York Jets, 31–21, with the trio of Keith Jackson, Howard Cosell, and Don Meredith in the broadcast booth, *Monday Night Football* began what has been one of the longest-running shows in television history.

"The start of *Monday Night Football* on ABC in 1970 is perhaps the most impactful sports innovation in the second half of the 20th century," said longtime NFL executive Joe Browne. "It was precedent-setting to have a weekly series of sports on prime time television. Back in those days, there were only three major networks and to have three hours a week on the prime time schedule of one of those networks was an idea that many, many TV executives could not conceive."

One of the major selling points of the Monday night package was that all the games would be televised in full color. It's easy to take that for granted today, but it was significant at the time. It was also significant that the NFL now had all three networks—ABC, CBS, and

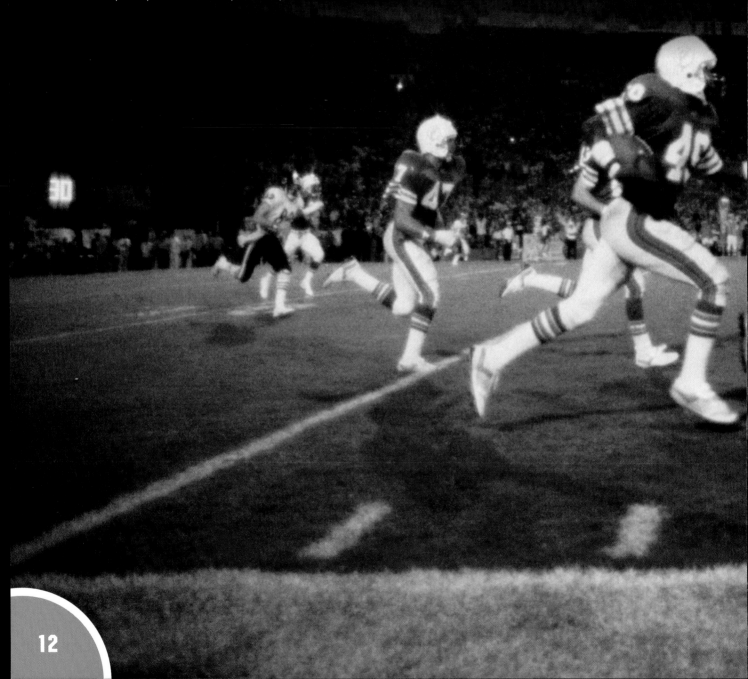

NBC—promoting NFL games each week on the networks other non-sports TV programming. This helped drive a wider audience, including female viewers, to the NFL for the first time.

In a time when there was no ESPN—or cable TV of any kind—halftime of the *Monday Night Football* game was often the first time many fans saw highlights of the games that had been played on Sunday.

"During the '70s, I didn't always stay up for Dandy Don singing 'Turn Out The Lights,' but I never missed Howard Cosell narrating the halftime highlights," recalled longtime NFL writer Jarrett Bell. "Must-see TV,

and it reflected the NFL as cultural institution.

Another appeal of *Monday Night Football*, especially in the decades before satellite TV paved the way for DirecTV's Sunday Ticket package, was that it was the rare opportunity for fans to see out-of-market teams.

"We can sit here and talk about the Greatest Game Ever Played and Joe Namath's guarantee in Super Bowl III, but the fact that 'appointment viewing' was created around the NFL by *Monday Night Football* is to me reason number one why the NFL has captured the fancy of America," said NFL Network's Rich Eisen. "Because America was captured by *Monday Night Football*."

The Dolphins-Bears 1985 matchup remains the highest rated *Monday Night Football* game in history.

8 THE CATCH

JANUARY 10, 1982

The 1981 NFC Championship Game was a symbolic changing of the guard. When Joe Montana scrambled to his right and lofted a game-winning touchdown pass into the outreached hands of Dwight Clark in the back of the end zone, it signaled the beginning of a new dynasty. Two weeks later, the San Francisco 49ers won the first of four Super Bowls in a nine-year span, all with Montana at the helm.

The 49ers' victory also signaled the beginning of the end of a long run of success for the Dallas Cowboys. Dallas became America's Team by getting to the Super Bowl five times in the '70s (winning twice), but The Catch marked the Cowboys' second straight loss in the NFC title game. They would actually reach the NFC title game a third year in a row, only to lose to the rival Redskins. While the 49ers continued their upward trajectory through the '80s, the Cowboys went in the opposite direction. They wouldn't return to relevance until Jimmy Johnson and Troy Aikman came along in the early '90s.

Things could easily have turned out different. The 1981 NFC title game was a back-and-forth affair, with Dallas taking a 27–21 lead midway through the fourth quarter thanks to a touchdown pass from Danny White to tight end Doug Cosbie. The 49ers' next possession was stalled when Montana was intercepted by Everson Walls, but San Francisco got the ball back one more time, starting a drive on their own 11-yard line with 4:54 left in the game.

The legend of Joe Montana had yet to take shape, but this drive marked the beginning of the narrative. In a classic display of Bill Walsh's West Coast offense, the 49ers chipped away with a mix of runs and short passes. Lenvil Elliott carried the ball four times for 30 yards. Receiver Freddie Solomon's 14-yard run on a reverse was the longest play of the drive. With 58 seconds left to play, the 49ers faced a third-and-3 from the Dallas 6-yard line.

The 49ers ran a play called "Sprint Right Option," which was designed to go to Solomon. Montana had found Solomon for a touchdown earlier in the game using this play. This time, however, Solomon slipped and the timing of the play was ruined. Dallas defenders Ed "Too Tall" Jones, Larry Bethea, and D.D Lewis chased Montana as the quarterback scrambled toward the right sideline. Montana pump-faked once, then lofted the ball into the back corner of the end zone. The ball was high enough to avoid the reach of Walls, who had good coverage on the play. But the 6-foot-4 Clark was able to leap high enough to get his hands on the ball and come down with the game-winner.

What a lot of fans might forget about this game is that it wasn't over after The Catch. Dallas had 51 seconds left and all they needed was a field goal to win. On first down from their 25, White hit Drew Pearson for a 31-yard gain—and it might have been a 75-yard touchdown if not for a game-saving tackle by Eric Wright. The Cowboys were on the 49ers' 44 with 38 seconds left. On the next play, however, San Francisco defensive end Lawrence Pillers forced White to fumble. Jim Stuckey recovered, and the 49ers were Super Bowl-bound. Two weeks later, they defeated the Cincinnati Bengals, 26–21, in Super Bowl XVI.

9 BREAKING THE COLOR BARRIER

MARCH 21, 1946

Halfback Kenny Washington (running with the ball) signed with the Los Angeles Rams, becoming the first African American player in the modern era. While Washington was technically the first to sign, he was one of four African Americans to break the color barrier that season—a year before Jackie Robinson made his major-league baseball debut. End Woody Strode signed with the Rams on May 7. In August, guard Bill Willis and running back Marion Motley signed with the Cleveland Browns of the All-American Football Conference, which began play that year and merged with the NFL four years later.

While Washington and Strode had limited success with the Rams, Motley and Willis both ended up in the Pro Football Hall of Fame. But all four had a collectively profound impact on the future of the sport.

Ironically, Washington was a teammate of Jackie Robinson on both the baseball and football teams at UCLA. Washington actually had a higher batting average than Robinson, but football was his real talent. In 1939, his senior season at UCLA, Washington led the nation in total offense.

The Bears' George Halas, who coached Washington in the college all-star game after that season, lobbied hard for the NFL to re-integrate so that Washington could play, but he was unsuccessful. When the Cleveland Rams relocated to Los Angeles for the 1946 season, the city insisted the NFL integrate as a condition for letting the Rams play in the Los Angeles Coliseum. As a result, the Rams signed Washington, who had become a big draw playing semi-pro ball in Los Angeles, and his UCLA teammate Strode.

Washington only played three seasons in the NFL—knee injuries had slowed him down before he ever joined the Rams—but he did make his presence felt. He averaged 7.4 yards per carry in 1947, leading the NFL in that category. His 92-yard touchdown that year remains the longest TD run in Rams history.

Strode, meanwhile, only played one season in the NFL but then made a name for himself in Hollywood. In 1960, Strode was nominated for a Golden Globe for a supporting role in the Kirk Douglas classic *Spartacus*.

10 RED GRANGE'S PRO DEBUT, BARNSTORMING TOUR

NOVEMBER 26, 1925

Just five days after playing his final college football game for the University of Illinois, superstar halfback Harold "Red" Grange made his debut with the Chicago Bears. College football was much more popular than pro football at the time, so Grange's signing was a major coup for the fledgling NFL. The Thanksgiving Day game between the Bears and the Chicago Cardinals drew a sold-out crowd of 36,000, establishing Grange as the league's first major gate attraction.

Ten days later, a crowd twice that size filled New York's Polo Grounds to see Grange and the Bears play the Giants. The Bears won, 19–7, but in the long run, this game was a significant victory for New York.

Tim Mara had been awarded the New York franchise at the start of the 1925 season for a mere $500. Despite the bargain-basement price, Mara was having financial difficulties with the team that first season and had been thinking about shutting down operations. The buzz created by the Red Grange visit played a key role in Mara's decision to keep with it.

After the '25 season ended, Grange and the Bears went on a barnstorming tour across the country—exposing tens of thousands of new fans to the NFL product. The player known as the "Galloping Ghost" later helped the Bears win a pair of NFL titles in the early 1930s, but his value to the NFL was perhaps at its greatest in those first few months as a pro.

11 ROZELLE BECOMES COMMISSIONER

JANUARY 26, 1960

When Pete Rozelle became the league's compromise choice—on the 23rd ballot—to replace Bert Bell as NFL commissioner, nobody could have predicted that he was about to embark on perhaps the most successful run that any commissioner of any professional sport has ever had. That is precisely what happened.

Bell suffered a fatal heart attack on October 11, 1959, appropriately while attending an Eagles-Steelers game (at different times, Bell had been a part-owner in both those teams). With the league's owners unable to name a consensus replacement for Bell, they settled on Rozelle, the 33-year-old general manager of the Los Angeles Rams. A public relations man by trade, Rozelle's 29 years as NFL commissioner saw the public face of the league skyrocket. He presided over the AFL-NFL merger, the birth and enormous growth in popularity of the Super Bowl, and the explosion of televised football.

"Pete Rozelle during his time as commissioner understood the impact of television better than anyone in the entertainment industry," said longtime NFL executive Joe Browne. "He convinced all the owners to pool their TV rights into one league package, and made certain that all road games were televised back to the visiting team's market."

Rozelle was much more than just a "PR guy," but he was a master promoter. He recognized very early on that the Super Bowl had the potential to be a national—and even international—spectacle. His PR hat played a key role in developing various events and catering to the media, all of which led to the concept of "Super Bowl Week" and created the enormous buzz of anticipation that made the Super Bowl an unofficial national holiday.

"The Super Bowl was started and nurtured on Pete's watch," said Browne.

In 1999, three years after his death, Rozelle was named by *The Sporting News* as the 20th century's most powerful person in sports.

"I don't think the league would be what it is without him," said Jim Steeg, who was hired by Rozelle in 1979 and worked at the NFL for 35 years. "He had a way of motivating you to do things not because of any other reason than you wouldn't want to disappoint him. And to me that's one of those great leadership skills that really the best have."

12 SUPER BOWL LI: THE COMEBACK

FEBRUARY 5, 2017

The New England Patriots of the 21st century appear many times in this book, as they should. With so many opportunities to honor them, why is Super Bowl LI their high-water mark? There are actually several good reasons:

- Bill Belichick won his fifth Super Bowl as head coach, breaking a tie with Pittsburgh's Chuck Noll for the NFL record.
- Tom Brady was named Super Bowl MVP for the fourth time, also a new record (breaking a tie with his boyhood idol, Joe Montana).
- The game featured the greatest comeback in Super Bowl history, as the Patriots were down 28–3 late in the third quarter when New England came storming back.
- After New England scored 25 points in the span of 15 minutes, the world was treated to the first overtime in Super Bowl history.

Brady completed 43 of 62 pass attempts for 466 yards—all three numbers Super Bowl records. Unlikely hero James White scored his second touchdown of the night with 57 seconds left in regulation and then Brady found Danny Amendola for the 2-point conversion that forced overtime.

Once the overtime period began, the Patriots' victory was a *fait accompli*. New England had all the momentum and the Falcons were gassed. The Patriots won the coin toss, started a drive at their 25, and proceeded to march down the field. Eight plays later, White scored his third touchdown of the game and New England had its fifth Lombardi Trophy.

13 SUPER BOWL I
JANUARY 15, 1967

It wasn't called the Super Bowl. That name had yet to be conceived. The AFL-NFL World Championship Game was actually the first game ever played between teams of both leagues. The NFL champion Green Bay Packers defeated the AFL champ Kansas City Chiefs,

35–10, before a crowd of 61,946 at Los Angeles Memorial Coliseum. Packers players received a $15,000 bonus for the win.

The NFL's owners couldn't fathom the idea of losing to the upstart AFL, and they made sure Packers coach Vince Lombardi knew how they felt.

"They wouldn't let Vince alone," his wife, Marie Lombardi, told *Pro! Magainze*. "They kept reminding him how much was at stake. I don't mean that as criticism. It was rather an attitude of, 'Thank God you're representing us in this game that means so much.' It was

gratifying they'd think that way and Vince appreciated it. But it amounted to more and more pressure."

The players felt it, too. Packers safety Willie Wood later said that they were getting letters and telegrams from players around the NFL stressing the importance of this game.

"As the kickoff got closer, the pressure reached an incredible peak," Wood told *Pro! Magazine*.

And the pressure continued through much of the first half. It was a close game at halftime, with the Packers holding a slim 14–10 lead. Green Bay's defense wasn't used to seeing the play-action passing that was run by Len Dawson and the Kansas City offense.

At halftime, they made a conscious decision to blitz Dawson more in the second half.

Four plays into the third quarter, Dawson rushed a pass to avoid a blitzing linebacker and Wood picked him off, returning the interception 50 yards to the Chiefs' 5-yard line. Elijah Pitts scored on the next play and the Packers never looked back.

When the game ended, the Packers knew they had beaten a worthy opponent.

"You could practically hear the giant sigh of relief in the dressing room," said Wood. "Then we started celebrating."

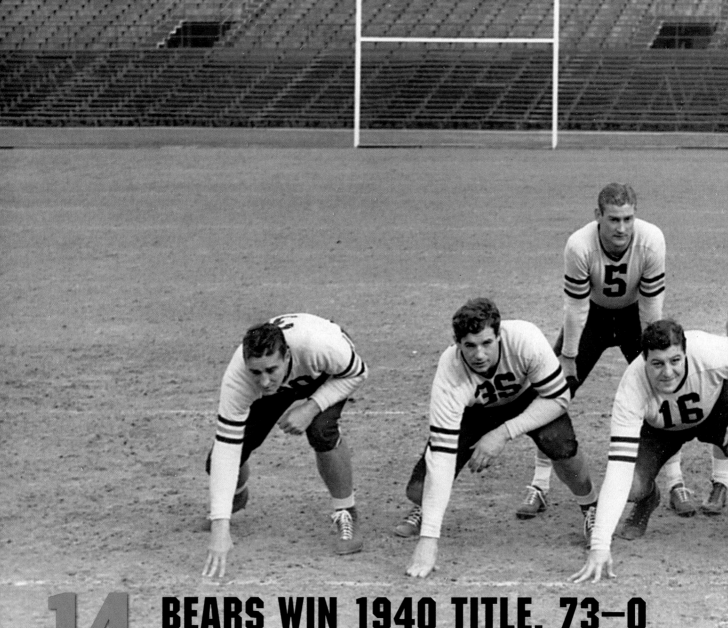

14 BEARS WIN 1940 TITLE, 73–0

The 1940 NFL Championship Game was more than just the most lopsided title game in league history. The Chicago Bears' 73–0 win over the Washington Redskins in Washington's Griffith Stadium was significant for other reasons.

For starters, it was the first championship game carried on network radio, with Hall of Fame broadcaster Red Barber calling the game to 120 stations around the country.

More importantly, it highlighted the Bears' use of the T formation offense, with three running backs lined up behind quarterback Sid Luckman in the backfield. The T formation was more popular in college football, and

Stanford University had just completed an undefeated season using it under head coach Clark Shaughnessy. Bears owner/coach George Halas brought in Shaughnessy to work with his team, and the results were immediate.

But it was more than just strategy and skill that propelled the Bears (pictured above) to victory. They were highly motivated on this day.

Believe it or not, the Redskins had defeated the Bears, 7–3, just three weeks prior to the title game. Redskins owner George Preston Marshall told reporters after that game that the Bears players were crybabies and quitters. It was perhaps the first example in NFL history of the term "bulletin board material"—and Halas

made sure to share with his players newspaper articles quoting Marshall.

"During the next three weeks, Halas kept reminding us of that defeat," Bears Hall of Fame end Dan Fortmann told *Pro! Magazine* in 1973. "I played a lot of times when we were inspired, but the team that took the field that day was the highest emotionally keyed squad I ever saw."

The Bears had an emotional advantage, a strategic advantage, and, apparently, a talent advantage. Running back Bill Osmanski ran 68 yards for a touchdown on Chicago's second play from scrimmage. Often having one of their three backs in motion before the snap, the Bears had Washington's defense confused all game. It was 28–0 at halftime, and then Chicago's defense took over. The Bears recorded eight interceptions in the game. In the third quarter alone, they returned three interceptions for touchdowns.

When it was over, the Bears had amassed 501 yards of total offense, 382 on the ground. Ten different players scored for the Bears; Luckman had a touchdown run and two TD passes. It was the Bears' second NFL championship victory and the first of four straight NFL Championship Game appearances for Chicago.

15 LOMBARDI NAMED PACKERS COACH

JANUARY 28, 1959

The Green Bay Packers finished 1–10–1 in 1958. This wasn't particularly newsworthy—it had been 12 years since the last time Green Bay finished with a winning record. So the expectations weren't necessarily very high when New York Giants offensive coordinator Vince Lombardi (seen here with Paul Hornung) was named the new Packers head coach on January 28, 1959.

Lombardi grew up in Brooklyn, New York, and played college football at Fordham University in the Bronx. Green Bay, Wisconsin, seemed an odd landing place for this gruff New Yorker, but he was 45 years old and still desperate to get his first head coaching job in the NFL. He took what he could get.

Lombardi immediately set the tone for a new era in team history. He instilled a rigorous practice regimen that paid immediate dividends. The Packers improved to 7–5 in 1959, earning Lombardi Coach of the Year honors. Of course, that was just the start.

Lombardi's Packers reached the NFL Championship Game six times between 1960 and '67, winning five NFL titles—culminating with the first two Super Bowls. In just 10 seasons as head coach, Lombardi's overall career record was 105–35–6—his winning percentage of .750 is easily the best of any NFL coach with at least 100 victories.

Lombardi died of cancer on September 3, 1970. So profound was the mark he left on the game that the Super Bowl trophy was renamed the Vince Lombardi Trophy just seven days later.

Cam Newton celebrates a touchdown during the second half of an October 2018 game against the Eagles.

16

CHIEFS WIN SUPER BOWL IV

JANUARY 11, 1970

The AFL scored a major victory when Joe Namath and the Jets stunned the Baltimore Colts in Super Bowl III, but a majority of NFL backers chalked that game up to a fluke. Couldn't happen again, they maintained. Which is why the Kansas City Chiefs' victory in Super Bowl IV was such a big deal.

The 1969 season was to be the last for the AFL, with the merger taking full effect in 1970. Thus, Super Bowl IV, played at Tulane Stadium in New Orleans, was a last hurrah for the upstart league. And while the Jets were the reigning world champions, there was little expectation of an AFL repeat. The Chiefs featured a stifling defense that allowed less than 13 points per game during the regular season. They held the Jets to six points in an AFL playoff win and the Raiders to seven in the AFL title game. Still, they entered Super Bowl IV as 12-point underdogs to the NFL's Minnesota Vikings.

Of course, not everyone was writing off the Chiefs. NFL Films boss Ed Sabol had Chiefs head coach Hank Stram wear a wireless microphone for the contest. Not that Sabol expected Kansas City to win, but he knew Stram would be more entertaining than stoic Vikings head coach Bud Grant.

What ensued was television gold. Stram not only gave NFL Films one of its signature moments, but Kansas City dominated the game. Hall of Fame quarterback Len Dawson was named MVP following the Chiefs' 23–7 victory, but it was Kansas City's swarming defense that ruled the day. Six members of the Chiefs' 1969 defense—tackles Curley Culp and Buck Buchanan, linebackers Willie Lanier and Bobby Bell, cornerback Emmitt Thomas, and safety Johnny Robinson—all went on to the Pro Football Hall of Fame.

17

DAWN OF AMERICA'S TEAM

JANUARY 16, 1972

The Dallas Cowboys franchise began play in 1960 and methodically developed into a well-oiled machine. They challenged for the NFL title a few times in the late '60s, then lost to the Baltimore Colts in Super Bowl V. When they made it back to the Super Bowl a year later, the Miami Dolphins were no match. Led by Super Bowl MVP Roger Staubach, the Cowboys cruised to a 24–3 victory. It was the first of two Super Bowls the Cowboys won in the '70s, a decade in which the team's popularity across the nation skyrocketed. Eventually, they simply became known as America's Team.

Technically, the Dallas Cowboys didn't become known as America's Team until after the 1978 season, but we'll use Super Bowl VI as a launch point because it was the start of the team's decade of dominance.

When the 1978 season ended, the Cowboys were coming off their fifth Super Bowl appearance in nine years. When NFL Films editor Bob Ryan was putting together the Cowboys' official 1978 highlight reel, he was trying to figure out what to name it. While scanning the footage NFL Films had gathered, Ryan couldn't help but notice that diehard fans in Cowboys gear showed up no matter where the team was playing. They seemingly had fans everywhere—thus, "America's Team" was born.

Of course, the team had to approve anything NFL Films was to put out. Naturally, Cowboys general manager Tex Schramm loved the name. Dallas head coach Tom Landry? Not so much.

"Tex was all for it—he thought that was great," recalls Gil Brandt, the Cowboys' VP of player personnel from 1960 to 1989. "Tom didn't like it very much because of the fact that now every time we went to play someplace, we'd hear, 'Oh, here comes America's Team . . .'

"Tex won out."

Landry did his level best to help his team rise to the pressure and meet those lofty expectations on the field. The ramifications of being America's Team, meanwhile, produced a windfall profit off the field in terms of merchandise sales. As Brandt recalls, he and Schramm knew early on that they had something special. They saw the bushels of fan mail their players were getting, and made a point to reply to all. The return envelope would include a 4x6 player photo, along with an order form for Cowboys merchandise.

"We did it ourselves for a while, then it became too big for us, so we gave it to a local sporting goods store," says Brandt. "Then it became too big for them to do, and Sears took it over."

At one point, Cowboys merchandise represented 50 percent of all NFL merchandise sold. Few nicknames in sports were more appropriate than "America's Team."

18

JIM BROWN'S HALL OF FAME CAREER COMES TO AN END

JULY 13, 1966

When Jim Brown announced his retirement from the NFL, he was the league's all-time leading rusher. He was coming off a 1965 season in which he rushed for 1,544 yards—the eighth time in his nine-year career that he led the NFL in rushing. And he was just 30 years old.

Imagine if Brown had played just a few more seasons? Would Walter Payton have passed his all-time record? Would Emmitt Smith have gotten there? We'll never know. Still, it's hard to say there has ever been a more dominant football player in NFL history. Brown rushed for 12,312 career yards with a combination of athleticism and brute force that made him so hard to tackle. He averaged 5.3 yards per carry.

Why did Brown retire at such a young age? It coincided with his interest in starting a second career in Hollywood. As the summer of '66 began, Brown was busy filming *The Dirty Dozen*, alongside the likes of Ernest Borgnine, Charles Bronson, and Donald Sutherland. With production falling behind schedule, it was clear Brown was going to miss the start of training camp. Browns owner Art Modell threatened to fine him for the days he missed . . . so Brown just decided to call it quits and focus on his acting career.

19

SUPER BOWL XXV | WIDE RIGHT

JANUARY 27, 1991

Super Bowl XXV in Tampa, Florida, offered a brief diversion from the Gulf War combat that had been taking place in the Middle East. It was the first time that bomb-sniffing dogs and metal detectors greeted fans at the Super Bowl. Once inside Tampa Stadium, however, fans were treated to one of the best and closest Super Bowls in NFL history.

Even before the opening kickoff, the tone was set with an inspiring performance of the National Anthem by Whitney Houston. Once the game began, New York Giants head coach Bill Parcells and defensive coordinator Bill Belichick presided over a classic game plan that needed to be flawless if the Giants were to have any chance against the heavily favored Buffalo Bills.

Buffalo had torn through the NFL that season, with quarterback Jim Kelly and running back Thurman Thomas posting big numbers in the "K-Gun" offense. The Giants, meanwhile, were relying on backup quarterback Jeff Hostetler, who took the reins after starting QB Phil Simms suffered a season-ending leg injury late in the season.

The Giants' plan was simple: pound the ball with running back Ottis Anderson, keep the ball away from the Bills' offense as much as possible, and when the Bills do go on offense, let Thomas do what he wants in the running game but flood the secondary and hit the receivers early and often.

The plan worked to perfection yet the game still hung in the balance. Anderson rushed for over 100 yards. The Giants dominated time of possession. Still, the Bills trailed by just one point with time for one last drive. Sticking to the game plan, the Giants were content to let Thomas slash his way across the field. As the game neared its end, Thomas had quietly racked up 135 rushing yards (he also had 55 receiving yards). Thomas' last run put Buffalo on the Giants' 29-yard line with eight seconds left.

Bills kicker Scott Norwood lined up for the 47-yard field goal, but the attempt sailed wide right. Final score: Giants 20, Bills 19. It remains the only Super Bowl ever decided by one point.

20

ALMOST-PERFECT PATRIOTS

2007

The 2007 Patriots featured one of the most prolific offenses in NFL history as they rolled to the league's first-ever 16–0 record in the regular season. Tom Brady set a single-season record with 50 touchdown passes. Randy Moss had an NFL-record 23 TD receptions. New England scored 589 points, the most ever in a season. The perfect regular season, however, was followed by a very imperfect ending.

First, the team was rocked by reports of cheating—the Patriots were accused of stealing opponents' sideline signals. For all the records New England set during the regular season, "Spygate" was all anyone wanted to talk about during the two weeks leading up to Super Bowl XLII in Glendale, Arizona. Still, they were heavily favored to win the title, as the New York Giants seemed to come out of nowhere to win the NFC that year.

In fact, the stage was set for a Giant upset during Week 17 of the regular season. The Giants were locked into the No. 5 seed in the playoffs. With nothing to play for, then-Giants head coach Tom Coughlin was under pressure to rest some injured starters before the playoffs. Instead, they laid out in an effort to hand the Patriots their first loss of the season. New England held on to win a thriller, 38–35, and cap the NFL's first 16–0 season.

It was a rare case of a team actually gaining momentum from a loss. The Giants won three straight road games in the playoffs to earn a rematch in the Super Bowl. Unlike the offensive fireworks that took place in Week 17, Super Bowl XLII was a defensive struggle. After averaging 36.8 points per game in the regular season, the Patriots were clinging to a 14–10 lead over the Giants as time ran down in the fourth quarter.

The Giants began their final drive on their own 17-yard line with 2:42 to play. The game-winning drive lasted 12 plays and 83 yards, but there is only one play anyone thinks about: on third-and-5 from the Giants' 44-yard line, Eli Manning dodged multiple Patriots pass rushers before finally launching a pass down the middle of the field. Giants receiver David Tyree out-jumped Patriots Pro Bowl safety Rodney Harrison for the ball—pinning it against his helmet as he came down to the turf.

The "Helmet Catch" gave New York first down at the Patriots' 24-yard line. Four plays later, Manning hit Plaxico Burress for the game-winning 13-yard touchdown. New England had one last desperation possession, but could not convert.

The New York Giants stunned the heavily-favored Patriots, 17–14.

21 IMMACULATE RECEPTION

DECEMBER 23, 1972

It remains one of the most romanticized plays in NFL history, even though the Immaculate Reception did not win a championship or even set up a title run. The play has become synonymous with the Pittsburgh Steelers dynasty of the '70s—yet it occurred a full two years before their first Super Bowl.

But it was certainly significant. In nearly 40 years of existence, the Steelers had never won a playoff game. It looked like that would remain the case as they trailed the Oakland Raiders, 7–6, with less than 30 seconds left in their AFC divisional playoff game at Three Rivers Stadium.

Facing fourth-and-10 at their own 40-yard line, Terry Bradshaw scrambled away from pressure and threw the ball about 30 yards downfield toward Steelers halfback John "Frenchy" Fuqua. Raiders safety Jack Tatum arrived just as the ball did, and the hit sent the ball flying backwards. Just before it touched the ground, Steelers running back Franco Harris scooped it up and raced 42 yards for the game-winning touchdown.

The Steelers lost to Miami in the AFC Championship Game one week later, but that wouldn't detract from the magnitude of the play.

"It's the miracle play that everybody remembers, and it kind of did introduce the Steelers to everyone," said veteran sportswriter Ray Didinger. "That was the day the Steelers came out of the shadows—a team that had never won anything."

The Raiders got a minor level of revenge by defeating Pittsburgh in the 1973 playoffs. In 1974, the Steelers beat the Raiders in the AFC Championship Game before winning the first of their four Super Bowl titles in the 1970s. Harris, who caught the Immaculate Reception, was MVP of Super Bowl IX.

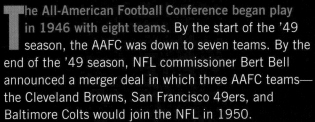

22 NFL–AAFC MERGER
DECEMBER 9, 1949

The All-American Football Conference began play in 1946 with eight teams. By the start of the '49 season, the AAFC was down to seven teams. By the end of the '49 season, NFL commissioner Bert Bell announced a merger deal in which three AAFC teams—the Cleveland Browns, San Francisco 49ers, and Baltimore Colts would join the NFL in 1950.

To be sure, there was really one main reason anyone was interested in the AAFC. Two days after the merger announcement, the Cleveland Browns won their fourth consecutive AAFC title. Led by team founder and owner Paul Brown and quarterback Otto Graham, the Browns were eager to challenge the best the NFL had to offer.

Fittingly, the 1950 season kicked off with a game between the Browns and the two-time defending NFL champion Philadelphia Eagles. Before a crowd of more than 71,000 in Philadelphia, Cleveland throttled the Eagles, 35–10, serving notice that the dominant team of the AAFC was ready to establish itself as a dynasty in the NFL.

Just three months after that, the Browns defeated the Giants in a playoff game to win the National Conference, then beat the Los Angeles Rams in the NFL Championship, 30–28.

In addition to the Browns, Colts, and 49ers joining the NFL, players from the four remaining AAFC teams that were folding were put into a "dispersal draft"—thus infusing some new talent into the NFL. There were already several future Hall of Famers on the Browns, the 49ers had running back Joe "the Jet" Perry, and the Colts had Y.A. Tittle. It's also worth noting that Elroy "Crazylegs" Hirsch got his start with the AAFC's Chicago Rockets, and Giants Hall of Famer Arnie Weinmeister started his career with the AAFC's New York Yankees.

23

JOE MONTANA'S SUPER BOWL XXIII MAGIC

JANUARY 22, 1989

Cincinnati Bengals quarterback Boomer Esiason was standing on the sideline during the closing minutes of Super Bowl XXIII. The Bengals clung to a 16–13 lead over the San Francisco 49ers, and a camera crew gathered near Esiason. It was the crew that would be filming the annual "I'm going to Disney World!" commercial that traditionally featured the Super Bowl MVP and was a staple of the Super Bowl postgame for years. Esiason was going to be their guy. Then something happened.

Joe Montana happened.

After a Cincinnati field goal gave the Bengals a 16–13 lead with 3:20 left, San Francisco started the ensuing drive on its own 8-yard line. Montana and the 49ers had won their first Super Bowl eight years earlier, also against the Bengals. The highlight of that game was a goal-line stand by the Niners. This time, it was the offense that took center stage. With cool precision, Montana drove the 49ers 92 yards—capping

the game-winning drive with a 10-yard scoring pass to receiver John Taylor with 34 seconds left to play.

As the 49ers players celebrated on their sideline, Esiason looked behind him, to where the Disney crew was standing. They were gone. He looked to his left and there they were . . . sprinting to the other side of the field to find a 49er for the commercial.

The MVP of Super Bowl XXIII was Jerry Rice, who caught 11 passes for 215 yards and one touchdown, but it was Montana whose legend mushroomed thanks to that 92-yard game-winning drive. It was the third of his four titles as 49ers quarterback. And he made it look so easy.

In fact, part of the legend of Joe Cool is how he kept his teammates calm and focused as they huddled up to began that final possession. As the offense gathered around him waiting for some words of inspiration, Montana looked up and pointed toward the stands behind the end zone, and told his teammates that he saw comic actor John Candy.

24 FIRST NFL DRAFT
FEBRUARY 8, 1936

It was then-Philadelphia Eagles owner Bert Bell, who would later be commissioner, who proposed the idea of an NFL draft in which teams chose players in reverse order of their record the previous year.

The first draft took place at the Ritz-Carlton in Philadelphia, and the first overall pick was University of Chicago halfback and Heisman Trophy winner Jay Berwanger (seen here). Drafted by the Eagles and then having his rights traded to the Bears, Berwanger never played in the NFL. The Eagles traded him because they didn't think they could meet his salary demands—reportedly $1,000 per game. Bears owner George Halas thought he could negotiate with Berwanger, but they couldn't agree on a deal and Berwanger simply walked away from football.

The first pick to actually sign and play in the NFL was the second overall pick, University of Alabama quarterback Riley Smith, who played three seasons for the Redskins.

Of course, that first NFL draft wasn't anything closely resembling the major event it is today. Teams didn't have scouting departments—even if they did, there was a limited number of players available to draft. All eight NFL teams were required to submit nine names, thus creating a pool of 72 draft-eligible players for the nine rounds.

For the record, the 1936 Draft produced four future members of the Pro Football Hall of Fame: tackle Joe Stydahar (sixth overall pick, Bears), fullback Tuffy Leemans (second round, 18th overall, New York Giants), end Wayne Millner (eighth round, 65th overall, Boston Redskins), and guard Dan Fortmann (ninth round, 78th overall, Bears).

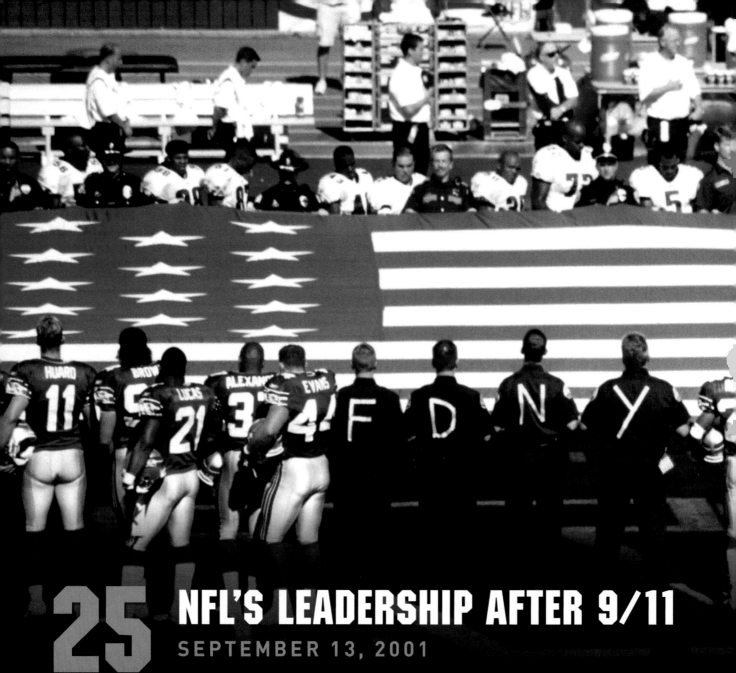

25 NFL'S LEADERSHIP AFTER 9/11

SEPTEMBER 13, 2001

Pete Rozelle once said that his greatest regret as NFL commissioner was not cancelling NFL games the week that President John F. Kennedy was assassinated. That wasn't lost on Rozelle's successor, Paul Tagliabue, immediately following the horrific terrorist attacks of September 11, 2001.

Two days after the 9/11 attacks that shook the nation, Tagliabue announced that all NFL games that week were postponed.

"There was a group arguing that you don't cave to a terrorist," recalled Tagliabue in explaining the league's thought process. "Ultimately, they realized this was different. You couldn't play a game with 3,000 people missing."

The weight of that decision was just part of the heavy responsibility that lay squarely on Tagliabue's

shoulders. In order to reschedule the postponed games (the week after the regular season was supposed to end) and still maintain the full playoff schedule, the NFL had to push the Super Bowl back one week—which meant negotiating with the National Auto Dealers Association to get them to move their convention, which had the Superdome and New Orleans hotel rooms booked that week. The commissioner also had to oversee the new security measures that were in place at every NFL stadium when fans returned on September 23, and he had to be a leader as his league's players and personnel did their part to help the nation heal.

"I think it's been lost by history what a big role Tagliabue had in leading the NFL through a crisis period," retired Pro Football Hall of Fame vice

president Joe Horrigan told *Sports Illustrated* in 2014. "I have always believed the actions he took following the attacks were critical not only for the NFL, but for America. The nation looked to its political leaders for strength and a sense of security. But we also looked to the private sector to help re-establish the all-important sense of normalcy that was taken from us all. I think his course of action became the template for crisis management in sports, and business."

Five months after the attacks, the American public was slowly getting back to a state of normalcy—though nothing would ever really be as it was. The Super Bowl would be a time to reflect on the tragedy that occurred when the season began and also show the world that the

The pregame show at the Louisiana Superdome featured Paul McCartney, the Boston Pops, and a video of all the living presidents and former First Lady Nancy Reagan reading speeches from Abraham Lincoln. During U2's goosebump-inducing halftime show, a giant screen scrolled the names of all the victims of the 9/11 attacks. At the show's end, Bono opened his jacket to reveal an American flag sewn inside it.

"I still think Super Bowl XXXVI is one of the biggest moments in the history of the league," said then NFL VP of Events Jim Steeg. "I just think if there's something the league should ever take credit for having really done well and making a difference in society, that would be it."

26

WALTER PAYTON PASSES JIM BROWN

OCTOBER 7, 1984

The Chicago Bears were a run-of-the-mill team through the first nine seasons of Walter Payton's NFL career. From 1975 to 1983, they only had two winning seasons. What they did have was one of the most dynamic running backs the league had ever seen. Nicknamed "Sweetness," Payton dazzled with smooth moves that left defenders frozen in their tracks. But he also defied that nickname at times, never afraid to run at a would-be tackler and get the better of the collision.

Payton rushed for at least 1,390 yards six times in his first nine seasons, including a league-best 1,852 yards in 1977, setting himself up to break the NFL's all-time rushing record in his 10th season. In Week 6 against the New Orleans Saints, Payton passed Jim Brown's total of 12,312, a mark that had stood for 19 years. Amazingly, Payton finished the '84 season with 1,684 rushing yards, the second-best total of his career.

More importantly, the Bears had turned the corner as a team and Payton finally found himself on a title contender. One year later, Payton rushed for 1,551 yards as Chicago finished 15–1 and cruised to a victory in Super Bowl XX. Sweetness was a champion.

When Payton retired after the 1987 season, he held NFL all-time records for carries (3,838), rushing yards (16,726), rushing touchdowns (110), and all-purpose yards (21,803).

27

SHULA WINS NO. 325

NOVEMBER 14, 1993

Unlike the modern-day trend of hiring head coaches at a young age, it was quite uncommon back in 1963. But Don Shula had made an impression in three seasons as defensive coordinator of the Detroit Lions—his only NFL coaching experience to that point. So the Baltimore Colts hired the 33-year-old Shula as their new head coach.

In seven seasons with the Colts, Shula racked up a 71–23–4 record and he led Baltimore to the 1968 NFL Championship. Unfortunately for Shula and the Colts, that was followed by the shocking loss to the New York Jets in Super Bowl III.

As it turned out, that stunning upset would be merely a footnote in Shula's Hall of Fame career. He became the Miami Dolphins head coach in 1970 and embarked on an extraordinary run of success. Shula presided over the perfect 1972 Dolphins, who went 14–0 in the regular season en route to winning Super Bowl VII. Miami repeated as champs a year later and continued to be a playoff fixture for another 20-plus seasons.

In all, Shula coached 33 years in the NFL—and had just two losing seasons. His coaching philosophy was always rooted in the emphasis on a strong running game—until, that is, he drafted quarterback Dan Marino in 1983. Shula willingly shifted his offense and thrived as Marino orchestrated the league's most prolific passing attack.

The wins continued to pile up, and when Miami defeated the Philadelphia Eagles, 19–14, on November 14, 1993, it was the 325th win of Shula's career, passing George Halas for tops on the all-time list.

Shula retired in 1995 with 347 career victories. Given the limited longevity of head coaches these days, it's easy to think Shula's mark will never be broken. Entering the 2019 NFL season, Patriots head coach Bill Belichick needed 55 wins to tie Shula, so he'd need to average 11 wins a season for five years, coaching until he's 71. If that doesn't happen, no other active coach is anywhere close.

28 PATRIOTS DYNASTY BORN

FEBRUARY 3, 2002

When the New England Patriots defeated the St. Louis Rams in Super Bowl XXXVI—the first time in Super Bowl history the game was decided on the final play—nobody could possibly have predicted it would be the beginning of one of the greatest dynasties in all of sports.

Adam Vinatieri's game-winning 48-yard field goal gave the Patriots a 20–17 win over the Rams, who had been favored in the game. It would be the first of three Super Bowl titles in a four-year span for New England,

and an unbelievable six championships over 18 years.

If the dynasty was officially born on this date, it had been conceived on September 23, 2001. That was the day that Jets linebacker Mo Lewis laid a vicious hit on Drew Bledsoe, knocking the Patriots' starting QB out for the season. Enter backup Tom Brady, a sixth-round draft pick in his second year.

Patriots fans—or anyone else, for that matter—could not have expected what was to come. Brady led his team to an 11–5 record and AFC East title. In the divisional

playoffs, New England came from behind against the Oakland Raiders in a driving snowstorm—aided by a controversial call that became known as the "Tuck Rule." As the Patriots were driving late in regulation, the Raiders thought they had forced a Brady fumble. Instead, officials ruled it an incomplete pass, and the drive culminated in Vinatieri's game-tying field goal. Another kick in the blinding snow, this time in overtime, sent the Patriots to the AFC title game, where they dispatched the Pittsburgh Steelers.

Before Super Bowl XXXVI even began, New England head coach Bill Belichick made an unprecedented decision that set the tone for the game. For the first time in Super Bowl history, rather than announcing individual players one-by-one to the crowd, Belichick's Patriots came running out of the tunnel together. As a team.

That unifying entrance symbolized the unselfishness and togetherness of the Patriots. And it introduced the world to a dynasty.

29

FIRST NATIONALLY
TELEVISED TITLE GAME

DECEMBER 23, 1951

The first nationally televised NFL game was broadcast by NBC in 1939, but NBC was still in its infancy back then. It wasn't until the 1950s when pro football on TV became popular, reaching critical mass when the Colts defeated the Giants in the 1958 Championship Game. But the first nationally televised title game was seven years prior to that.

The DuMont Network paid $75,000 for the rights to broadcast the game. DuMont was an early rival to major networks NBC and CBS, though it didn't have the deep pockets that the other two had. DuMont's popular TV shows included *Cavalcade of Stars* (hosted by Jackie Gleason), kids show *Captain Video and His Video Rangers*, and *The Ernie Kovacs Show*.

DuMont broadcast games during the 1951 regular season on a local or regional basis, but they broadcast the title game coast-to-coast. The Los Angeles Rams hosted the Cleveland Browns at the Los Angeles Coliseum. It was a rematch of the 1950 title game, when the Browns won their fifth consecutive title—their first in the NFL after dominating all four seasons of the All-American Football Conference.

The game was back and forth, eventually tied at 17 in the fourth quarter. With the Rams on their own 27-yard line, Hall of Fame quarterback Norm Van Brocklin found Hall of Fame receiver Tom Fears at midfield, and Fears raced past two defenders to complete a 73-yard touchdown. Final score: Rams 24, Browns 17.

The Rams had previously won an NFL title in 1945, their last season in Cleveland, and the St. Louis Rams won Super Bowl XXXIV. But the 1951 championship remains the Rams' only title in their combined 51 seasons in Los Angeles.

➤ Elroy "Crazylegs" Hirsch hauls in a pass.

Earl Campbell of the Houston Oilers runs through tacklers during a December 1979 game.

30 FIRST CHAMPIONSHIP GAME
DECEMBER 17, 1933

The 1933 season was the first in which the league was divided into two divisions, with the intention of pitting the division winners against each other in a championship game. The idea was the brainchild of Boston Redskins owner George Preston Marshall, a brilliant promoter in his day. His fellow owners approved the idea, and so the 1933 season began with two divisions. In the West were the Chicago Bears, Chicago Cardinals, Portsmouth, Green Bay, and Cincinnati. The East division included the Redskins, New York Giants, Brooklyn, Philadelphia, and Pittsburgh.

At season's end, the division winners were the Bears and Giants. A crowd of more than 20,000 came to Wrigley Field to see the hometown Bears capture that first championship game, 23–21.

The hero of the game was the Bears' legendary Bronko Nagurski, who on this day won the game with his arm.

A charter member of the Pro Football Hall of Fame, Nagurski threw a pair of touchdown passes. The bruising fullback from International Falls, Minnesota, was far more famous for his running and blocking—and that's

what made him a threat as a passer. With the football in his hands, defenses were too concerned that he'd be running at them.

"Bronko would buck up to the line and you'd have to come in to meet him as a linebacker," recalled Giants Hall of Famer Mel Hein in *Pro! Magazine*. "Then he'd stand straight up and lob a little pass. We all knew it was coming but we couldn't afford to concentrate on it because we couldn't afford to give Bronko any running room."

31 CONGRESS OKAYS SINGLE-NETWORK TV DEALS

SEPTEMBER 30, 1961

After the Baltimore Colts' overtime win against the New York Giants in the 1958 NFL Championship Game, the appetite for televised professional football became insatiable. Until then, TV networks worked with individual teams. Eventually, the NFL decided it would be better to pool its rights for all teams, creating an exclusive package. But when the NFL and CBS tried to broker such a deal, a court decision ruled that this strategy violated antitrust laws.

Fortunately for the NFL—and, really, for all interested parties—that decision was overruled by the "Sports Broadcasting Act of 1961."

President John F. Kennedy signed into law a

bill that legalized single-network television contracts by professional sports leagues. Known as the Sports Broadcasting Act, it allowed the NFL to sign big network deals.

The Sports Broadcasting Act had ramifications for all major sports, but it had its greatest effect on the NFL.

It allowed the league to create "packages" with a single network, a model that has been incredibly lucrative through the years. Today, of course, the league has deals with multiple networks by dividing the schedule into different packages—AFC, NFC, Monday night, etc. This 1961 decision paved the way.

32

OTTO GRAHAM'S LAST GAME . . . AND SEVENTH TITLE

DECEMBER 26, 1955

There can never be a debate about the greatest quarterback in NFL history without the inclusion of Otto Graham. You can talk about style of play or sensational stats, but Graham's resume speaks for itself: Ten seasons played. Ten championship games. Seven championship victories.

Perhaps detracting from Graham's legacy—or at least his perception in the modern era—is the fact that his first four titles with the Cleveland Browns were not in the NFL. The Browns were the marquee franchise in the upstart All-American Football Conference, winning the title in all four seasons of the league's existence. The AAFC folded after the 1949 season, with the Browns, San Francisco 49ers, and Baltimore Colts merging into the NFL in 1950. The Browns quickly established themselves as a power in their new league. In the 1950 NFL title game, Graham passed for 298 yards and four touchdowns, adding 99 yards rushing, in a 30–28 win over the Los Angeles Rams.

A year later, Graham won the first of his three NFL MVP Awards. In 1952, he led the NFL in passing yards and touchdowns.

Amazingly, Graham triumphantly rode off into the sunset not once but twice. Before the 1954 season, Graham told Paul Brown that he planned to retire at the end of the season. Cleveland made it back to the NFL title game, and Graham threw three touchdown passes and ran for three more scores in a 56–10 rout of the Detroit Lions. Graham announced his retirement after the game.

But wait, there's more . . . When Cleveland opened training camp in 1955, Brown was unsatisfied with the quarterbacks vying to fill Graham's shoes. So he called Graham and convinced him to come back for one more year.

Graham, who turned 34 by the end of the '55 season, won his third league MVP and led the Browns to the NFL Championship Game against the Los Angeles Rams. He threw two TD passes and ran for two more in a 38–14 victory at the Los Angeles Coliseum.

Overall, in 10 seasons split between the NFL and AAFC, Graham's record was 114–20–4, including 9–3 in the playoffs.

33 PRO FOOTBALL HALL OF FAME OPENS

SEPTEMBER 7, 1963

Being known as the birthplace of pro football would have been sufficient for the good people of Canton, Ohio. The downtown location where George Halas and others met in 1920 to formalize the organization that would become known as the National Football League remains etched in history. But when the league began to consider a location for its Hall of Fame in the late 1950s, Canton jumped at the opportunity.

The banner headline of the *Canton Repository* on December 6, 1959, declared: "PRO FOOTBALL NEEDS A HALL OF FAME AND LOGICAL SITE IS HERE." Thus began Canton's campaign to host the museum. One month later, William E. Umstattd of the Timken Company was chosen to make the city's formal bid to the NFL. Three months later, the bid was accepted and civic groups quickly raised nearly $400,000 to build the Hall.

When the Pro Football Hall of Fame opened its doors on September 7, 1963, it welcomed a charter class of 17 Hall of Famers. The Class of '63 included:

Sammy Baugh
Bert Bell
Joe Carr
Earl (Dutch) Clark
Harold (Red) Grange
George Halas
Mel Hein
Wilbur (Pete) Henry
Robert (Cal) Hubbard

Don Huston
Earl (Curly) Lambeau
Tim Mara
George Preston Marshall
John (Blood) McNally
Bronko Nagurski
Ernie Nevers
Jim Thorpe

The Class of 2019 brought the total to 326 members of the Hall. The one constant from 1963 to present day is the immense pride that Cantonites take in being home to the Hall. Literally thousands of residents from Canton and surrounding communities use their annual vacation time to work as volunteers during the week-long enshrinement celebration every summer.

"It's pretty incredible," said Joanne Murray, VP of community events and sponsorships, Canton Regional Chamber of Commerce. "We think for a city of our size to have that kind of commitment is really extraordinary."

For their part, many of the living members of the Hall—known as the Gold Jackets—return to Canton every summer. On the Friday of enshrinement weekend, they gather for the Ray Nitschke Luncheon, named for the Green Bay Packers Hall of Fame linebacker, a closed-door affair in which they remind the incoming class what a special fraternity they now belong to.

If they didn't already know that, the people of Canton are quick to remind them with their great respect and hospitality.

"They're so glad you're there," said Hall of Famer Joe DeLamielleure, the former Buffalo Bills offensive lineman. "People always ask if I'm coming back and I say, 'Are you kidding? I'm always coming back!'"

PRO FOOTBALL HALL OF FAME
CANTON, OHIO

34 AFL'S CHALLENGE

DECEMBER 6, 1963

While NFL commissioner Pete Rozelle is credited with engineering the AFL-NFL merger that triggered the Super Bowl era, perhaps there would never have been a Super Bowl if not for the challenge put forth by AFL commissioner Joe Foss.

The American Football League began play in 1960. If the upstart league didn't pose an immediate threat to the growing popularity of the NFL, it at least caught the attention of the senior circuit. The AFL started franchises in cities that were eager for pro football, they secured a national television contract, and enticed some big-name college football players to give them a try.

At the end of the AFL's fourth season in existence, Foss sent a letter to NFL commissioner Pete Rozelle in which he suggested a championship game between the winners of both leagues. "I feel strongly that the time has arrived for the inauguration of such an annual game," he wrote. Foss called for the first game to be played at the conclusion of the 1964 season. He was only off by two years; as part of the merger, the first AFL-NFL World Championship was played at the end of the 1966 season. Of course, that game is also recognized by another name—Super Bowl I.

Len Dawson and the Kansas City Chiefs take on the New York Jets during a November 1966 AFL game at Shea Stadium.

35 BIRTH OF THE PITTSBURGH STEELERS DYNASTY

JANUARY 12, 1975

The Pittsburgh Steelers have been one of the most consistent winners in the NFL since the early 1970s. It's hard to believe that they were once one of the league's most consistent losers, but that was indeed the case.

The Steelers had been part of the NFL since 1933. Art Rooney was among the most respected owners in the league. But his team? The Steelers were never a serious contender through their first four decades of existence—they had never won a playoff game.

Soon after they hired Chuck Noll in 1969, that all changed. While the Immaculate Reception in 1972 turned heads and made the football world take notice of these Steelers, their full-fledged arrival came in 1974.

It started with the draft that year. The Steelers' 1974 Draft class was historic, producing four future Hall of Famers: Lynn Swann (first round), Jack Lambert (second), John Stallworth (fourth), and Mike Webster (fifth). That quartet joined a team that already featured five other future Hall of Famers in Terry Bradshaw, Franco Harris, Joe Greene, Jack Ham, and Mel Blount.

After going 10–3–1 in the regular season, the Steelers beat Buffalo and Oakland in the playoffs before facing the Minnesota Vikings in Super Bowl IX. Played in New Orleans' Tulane Stadium, the Steel Curtain defense was dominant. Pittsburgh led 2–0 at halftime thanks to the first safety in Super Bowl history (Dwight White tackled Fran Tarkenton in the end zone). Franco Harris scored early in the third quarter to make it 9–0. Harris earned MVP honors as he rushed for 158 yards in a 16–6 victory.

With Noll presiding over a star-studded team, the Steelers would end up winning four Super Bowls in a six-year span.

36 NEW RULES TO CREATE MORE OFFENSE

MARCH 17, 1978

It's a running theme in the NFL that thet Competition Committee has consistently adjusted the rules of the game to benefit the offense. There are several examples of this over the years, but none more extreme than what took place following the 1977 season.

Two important new rules were implemented: 1) offensive linemen were allowed to extend their arms and grab defenders; and 2) defensive players could not hit receivers after five yards.

These new rules weren't created in a vacuum. The overall offensive woes of 1977 almost demanded that something be done.

In Week 1 of the '77 season, there were five shutouts. Thirteen teams scored 10 or fewer points. For the season, there were 25 shutouts. Fifteen of the league's 28 teams averaged 17 points or less per game.

Dallas Cowboys general manager Tex Schramm, one of the more influential members of the Competition Committee, pushed hard for the rule changes. And the results were readily apparent.

Before 1978, there was only one instance of a quarterback throwing for 4,000 yards in a season (Joe Namath, 1967). In the 10 years after the new rules, eight different quarterbacks topped 4,000 yards a total of 12 times.

"It brought a new dimension of passing into the league," said Dallas Cowboys Hall of Fame personnel director Gil Brandt. "It enabled teams that were down by 10 points with two minutes left to be able to come back. You couldn't do that running the football."

Steve Largent pulls in one of his
100 career receiving touchdowns.

37 MIRACLE AT THE MEADOWLANDS

NOVEMBER 19, 1978

It remains one of the NFL's most-viewed bloopers, but it is so much more than that. You've seen the play countless times. New York Giants quarterback Joe Pisarcik could have run out the clock to seal a victory over the Philadelphia Eagles. "Victory formation" was not yet a thing, but the quarterback could still take a step back from the line and just go down. Instead, Pisarcik made an awkward attempt to hand the ball off to fullback Larry Csonka. The resulting fumble bounced perfectly into the hands of Eagles cornerback Herman Edwards, who ran it in for the game-winning touchdown.

"I was stunned," recalled Giants Hall of Fame linebacker Harry Carson, then in his third season. "All we had to do was run out the clock. And the thing that I remember was that I was so stunned that I could not get up from the bench when the game was over. Players walk off the field, walk across the field to congratulate the other team. I was stuck in my seat and could not move."

In reality, it was the best thing that could have happened to the Giants, a storied NFL franchise that had been languishing for more than a decade. The front office was in shambles and the co-owners, Wellington Mara and nephew Tim Mara, did not see eye to eye. Had the Giants avoided that stunning loss to the Eagles, their record would have improved to 6–6. Regardless of what happened over the last four games of the season, chances are the Giants would have been content to carry on in mediocrity.

Instead, "The Fumble" proved to be the last straw for the franchise. The coaching staff and front office were fired. When the Mara family couldn't agree on a general manager, the league office stepped in and made them hire Dolphins personnel exec George Young . . . who would go on to rebuild the franchise and position the Giants to be one of the most successful teams in the league for the next 35 years.

Here's just a simple look at some of Young's first decisions running the team:

- He hired Ray Perkins, a Bear Bryant disciple and disciplinarian, as head coach.
- His first draft pick was unheralded Morehead State quarterback Phil Simms.
- A year later, he drafted Lawrence Taylor.
- When Perkins left to become head coach at his alma mater, Alabama, Young replaced him with a guy named Bill Parcells.

"I've heard some over the years say 'The Fumble' turned around the fate of the franchise, and I agree with that," said Simms. "It just made the Giants change how they run their football team, and it definitely made them better."

When you think about it, the Miracle at the Meadowlands had a profound effect on both franchises involved. The victory gave the Eagles a 7–5 record; they split their last four games in 1978 to finish 9–7 and earn a Wild Card berth—ending a 17-year playoff drought for the franchise. Had Philadelphia lost on that fateful day, it's easy to assume Dick Vermeil would not have taken his team to the playoffs that year.

But he did, and three years later, he had the Eagles in the Super Bowl.

"When you're a losing team, every win is a building block—and a win like that is two or three blocks," said Vermeil. "It's a great way to make sure your players always know they still have a chance to win."

38 NFL DRAFT ON ESPN
APRIL 29, 1980

Recognized now as the "global leader in sports," ESPN launched as a small cable startup in 1979. Today, they require multiple channels to carry all of their content. In the early days, however, they were starved for good programming. How starved? ESPN's Chet Simmons reached out to NFL commissioner Pete Rozelle with the crazy idea of televising the 1980 NFL Draft.

At the time, this concept seemed ridiculous. To that point, the NFL held its annual draft in a New York City hotel ballroom on a Tuesday morning. Nothing more than team reps sitting at tables and the small contingent of league employees running the meeting from the front of the room.

When Rozelle suggested to NFL owners that ESPN

down the idea. The draft was a private business meeting, they contended, fearing that making it a public event would open it up for agents to get involved.

In yet another example of Rozelle's status as a visionary, the commissioner found a way to make it happen. He went back to Simmons and told him that while ESPN can't broadcast the draft as an "event," the NFL couldn't stop him from covering it as news. So ESPN set up a desk in the corner of the ballroom, with a host and an analyst. Sure enough, fans were interested.

ESPN's coverage of the draft grew exponentially from there. The league moved it from a weekday event to the weekend, eventually stretching it to three days with the first round in prime time. ESPN's involvement has grown to the point where its parent company, ABC, televised the first round of the 2019 Draft in prime time.

39

EPIC IN MIAMI: CHARGERS-DOLPHINS PLAYOFF GAME

JANUARY 2, 1982

When the San Diego Chargers jumped out to a 24–0 lead over the Miami Dolphins in this divisional playoff game at the Orange Bowl, who could have imagined they were witnessing one of the greatest NFL games ever played? As the action continued, that fact became undeniable.

Dolphins head coach Don Shula pulled starting QB David Woodley in the second quarter, and backup Don Strock breathed life into the offense. Miami scored twice to make it 24–10 and had the ball at the San Diego 40-yard line with six seconds left before halftime. Shula called for a "hook and lateral" play—Strock found Duriel Harris on the right sideline at about the 25-yard line. Before he could be tackled, Harris flipped the ball to running back Tony Nathan, who had trailed the play, and Nathan streaked untouched down the sideline for a touchdown that made it a one-score game at halftime. It was a "ding ding" moment that set the tone for the nonstop drama that was to come.

Miami scored first in the third quarter to tie the game, only to see San Diego regain the lead when Hall of Fame quarterback Dan Fouts threw a 25-yard touchdown pass to Hall of Fame tight end Kellen Winslow. Strock came right back and threw a 50-yard TD pass to tie the game at 31.

Miami scored to take its first lead of the game at the start of the fourth quarter. They clung to that lead when San Diego got the ball at its own 18-yard line with 4:39 left in regulation. Fouts methodically drove the Chargers down the field. With 58 seconds left, Fouts hit James Brooks for a nine-yard touchdown that tied the game at 38. The Dolphins did manage to get to San Diego's 26-yard line before time expired, and Miami kicker Uwe Von Schamann attempted a 43-yard field goal to win the game—only to have it blocked by Winslow.

With both teams exhausted, the overtime period was more like a battle of attrition. Both teams missed field goal tries before San Diego's Rolf Benirschke finally converted a 29-yard kick with 1:08 left in the first overtime.

The enduring image from this game is of Winslow being carried off the field by his teammates after the win. It might have been the epitome of a player leaving everything he had on the field. Winslow caught 13 passes for 166 yards and a touchdown, in addition to the blocked kick that forced overtime. Winslow had to be treated throughout the game for a shoulder injury, dehydration, cramps, and a gash in his lip that required stitches.

"I have coached for 31 or 32 years and this is tremendous," Chargers head coach Don Coryell said after the game. "There has never been a game like this. It was probably the most exciting game in pro football history."

The aftermath of this game produced a cruel fate for that Chargers team, which remains one of the best teams of the Super Bowl era to have never reached the Super Bowl. The win in Miami sent San Diego to the AFC Championship Game for the second straight year. However, one week after playing this game in the heat of Miami, San Diego had to travel to Cincinnati, where an arctic blast created one of the coldest games in NFL history. In conditions that rivaled the Ice Bowl, the Bengals easily defeated the Chargers, 27–7, before losing to the 49ers in Super Bowl XVI.

The Chargers of Fouts and Coryell never got that close to another Super Bowl, but their epic playoff win in Miami will never be forgotten.

40

SLINGIN' SAMMY'S "TRIPLE CROWN"

1943

Sammy Baugh actually got his famous nickname—Slingin'—from his days as a third baseman on the Texas Christian University baseball team. Of course, Baugh was also a star quarterback at TCU, where he was a two-time All-American. In 1937, the Washington Redskins made him their first-round draft pick.

To say Baugh made an immediate impact in the NFL is an understatement. He led the league in passing that season, and then threw for 335 yards and three scores in the 1937 NFL Championship Game victory over the Bears. Baugh's 335 yards stood as the most by a rookie in a playoff game until Seattle's Russell Wilson topped it in 2012.

Baugh's Hall of Fame career was off and running. He led the league in passing yards four times and passer rating six times. But his most impressive accomplishment came in 1943, when the versatile Baugh had one of the best all-around seasons in NFL history.

The NFL was still in the two-way era during Baugh's playing days, and Baugh was not only an excellent defensive back but also one of the best punters in the NFL. When the 1943 season ended, Baugh led the league in passing (78.0 rating), punting (45.9 yard average), and interceptions (11). It's safe to say that triple crown feat will never be matched.

41 HALAS' LAST TITLE

DECEMBER 29, 1963

When the Chicago Bears defeated the New York Giants, 14–10, in the 1963 NFL Championship Game, it marked the sixth NFL title for George Halas in his 36th season as Bears head coach (and eighth as owner of the Bears). Not that Halas needed this win to cement his legacy. Three months earlier, he was a member of the inaugural class of the Pro Football Hall of Fame.

Forty-three years earlier, Halas had been in the room at the Hupmobile showroom in Canton when the National Football League was born. He represented the Decatur Staleys and took ownership of the team when he moved them to Chicago and renamed them the Bears in 1922. Few people know that Halas actually played for the Bears until 1929 (he scored 10 career touchdowns).

Halas was 51 years old when he coached the Bears to their seventh NFL championship . . . in 1946. It was their fourth title in seven years, and Halas was already a legendary figure in the league. He made it back to the title game in 1950—the year he became the first NFL coach to win his 200th game—but lost to the Los

Halas was 68 when he got the Bears back to the NFL Championship Game in 1963. It was a classic matchup of Chicago's "Monsters of the Midway" defense against the Giants' high-powered offense led by Y.A. Tittle (who set a new NFL record in 1963 with 36 TD passes), Del Shofner, and Frank Gifford.

Tittle found Gifford for a first-quarter touchdown, but the Bears' defense stiffened after that. Bill Wade had a pair of short touchdown runs and that's all Chicago needed. Tittle, who had been knocked around all day by the Bears' defense, had one last chance with time winding down, but he was intercepted in the end zone by Richie Petitbon with 10 seconds left.

Halas coached four more seasons, retiring at age 72. In 40 seasons as coach of the Bears, he only had six losing seasons. His 324 career victories stood as the all-time NFL record for 26 years, until Don Shula broke it, and he remains No. 2 on the list.

Halas' six NFL titles are the most by one coach, a record he shares with Curly Lambeau of the Packers and

42 RIGGO'S SUPER BOWL HEROICS

JANUARY 30, 1983

The Washington Redskins trailed the Miami Dolphins, 16–13, with 10:28 left to play in Super Bowl XVII when they faced a fourth-and-1 at the Miami 43-yard line. Despite the outward appearance that he was a mild-mannered, Southern gentleman, Washington head coach Joe Gibbs was really nothing if not ruthless when it came to calling his offense. So the plan to hand the ball off to John Riggins and have the bruising fullback run behind that giant Redskins offensive line for a first down was never really in question.

But Riggins—a.k.a. The Diesel—was in no mood to settle for a first down. Dolphins cornerback Don McNeal grabbed Riggins' jersey and tried to drag him down as the Redskins back came around the left side of the line. Riggins shed McNeal to the turf and began to pick up a head of steam—racing 43 yards down the sideline to paydirt before any other Dolphin defender could reach him.

The Redskins had their first lead of the game. After stopping Miami's ensuing possession, Washington capped its next possession with a clock-eating touchdown drive and capped a 27–17 Super Bowl victory. Riggins finished with 38 carries for a then–Super Bowl record 166 yards rushing, earning MVP honors.

Riggins' run is one of the most enduring Super Bowl images, and the symbol of the Redskins' first-ever Super Bowl title. It also marked the beginning of an incredible 10-year run for Washington. Gibbs led the Redskins to three Super Bowl titles in those 10 years—each time winning with a different starting quarterback.

Theismann was behind center for Super Bowl XVII. Five years later, Doug Williams was MVP of Super Bowl XXII over the Denver Broncos. Four years after that, it was Mark Rypien leading the way in Super Bowl XXVI over the Buffalo Bills.

43 SNEAKERS GAME

DECEMBER 9, 1934

Football equipment and apparel have evolved incredibly through the years, much more in the NFL's second half-century than its first. Yet one must go back 85 years to identify the one game in which gear played the greatest role in deciding a championship.

Before there was ever such a thing as the "frozen tundra" of Green Bay, the Chicago Bears and New York Giants played the 1934 NFL Championship Game in New York's Polo Grounds on a field that was so icy it was impossible for players on either team to get enough footing to make any big plays. The Bears, who won the title in 1933 and were 13–0 in the regular season, came into the game as heavy favorites to repeat. After a Bronko Nagurski one-yard touchdown run, the Bears managed to take a 10–3 lead into halftime.

It was Giants end Ray Flaherty, who would later become a Hall of Fame head coach with the Redskins, who suggested to Giants coach Steve Owen that players

might get better footing if they wore rubber-soled sneakers instead of the leather cleats. So Owen dispatched a team assistant to Manhattan College, where he got the athletic director to go through the lockers of the basketball team. By halftime, the assistant was back at the Polo Grounds with nine pairs of basketball sneakers . . . and it made all the difference in the world.

Chicago kicked a third-quarter field goal to go up 13–3, but New York owned the fourth quarter. Ken

Strong had a pair of touchdown runs while Ed Danowski had a touchdown pass and a touchdown run. The Giants scored 27 unanswered points to win 30–13 and take home the championship.

"We immediately said something was wrong, because they suddenly had good footing and we didn't," Nagurski said after the game. "They just out-smarted us."

Randy Moss hauls in a touchdown against the Dolphins in a 2008 game.

SIX TDS FOR SAYERS

Halfback Gale Sayers literally hit the ground running in his rookie season with the Chicago Bears. The first-round pick from Kansas set a then-NFL record with 22 touchdowns—and that mark remains the all-time rookie record. Six came in this one game against the San Francisco 49ers.

Sayers was the third player in NFL history to score six touchdowns in a game, joining Ernie Nevers (Chicago Cardinals, 1929) and Dub Jones (Cleveland Browns, 1951). Nobody has done it since.

Nevers' record performance on Thanksgiving Day was notable because he also kicked four extra points—accounting for all 40 points the Cardinals scored that day. Nevers' 40-point game is the longest-standing record in NFL history.

Sayers didn't kick any extra points, and he didn't account for all his team's touchdowns in that 61–20 win over the 49ers (among the other scoring, Mike Ditka had a 29-yard TD reception). But the player known as the "Kansas Comet" had one of the most electrifying performances ever.

Sayers opened the scoring that day when he took a screen pass and went 80 yards to paydirt. His next four scores were all on the ground, including a 50-yard run. And with the game well out of reach, Sayers scored his last touchdown on an 85-yard punt return.

Sayers touched the ball 11 times in the game, scoring six times. He finished with nine carries for 113 yards, two receptions for 89 yards, and five punt returns for 134 yards. He averaged 21 yards every time he touched the ball.

Sayers led the NFL in all-purpose yards in each of his first three seasons, and he led the league in rushing twice. Injuries cut his career short and he was forced to retire after just seven seasons. But he made such an impact on the game that in 1977 he became the youngest person (34) ever elected to the Pro Football Hall of Fame.

45 GREATEST DRAFT EVER
APRIL 26, 1983

Most teams have a particular draft they can look back on and point to as a pivotal moment for the franchise. In 1965, the Chicago Bears had a pair of first-round picks and used them to take two players that went on to become Hall of Famers—Gale Sayers and Dick Butkus. In 1974, the Pittsburgh Steelers drafted four players that reached the Hall: Lynn Swann (first round), Jack Lambert (second), John Stallworth (fourth), and Mike Webster (fifth).

But when it comes to the best overall draft, top to bottom, in NFL history, it's hard to compete with the 1983 Draft.

"When you look at it as far as All-Pros, Pro Bowlers, it was probably the best ever," says former Dallas Cowboys personnel exec Gil Brandt.

Much is made of the quarterbacks that were taken in the first round of the 1983 Draft, and rightfully so. Six quarterbacks in all were taken in Round 1—most ever in the first round of a draft. While John Elway, Jim Kelly, and Dan Marino ended up in the Pro Football Hall of Fame, Tony Eason started in the Super Bowl for the New England Patriots and Ken O'Brien played in the Pro Bowl for the New York Jets. And the quarterbacks were just part of the story.

Three other first-rounders went to the Hall of Fame: running back Eric Dickerson, offensive lineman Bruce Matthews, and cornerback Darrell Green. Chicago Bears Hall of Fame defensive end Richard Dent was an eighth-round pick—203rd overall.

But wait, there's more . . .

Other first-round notables who made their mark in the league were offensive tackle Chris Hinton (who was part of the blockbuster trade that sent Elway to the Denver Broncos after the Colts drafted him), running back Curt Warner, offensive tackle Jimbo Covert, and safety Joey Browner.

Round Two produced eight Pro Bowl players, including 49ers running back Roger Craig, Rams receiver Henry Ellard, Giants defensive end Leonard Marshall, and Bills linebacker Darryl Talley. The final pick of Round Three was Redskins Pro Bowl defensive end Charles Mann.

All in all, the 1983 Draft produced 42 Pro Bowl players, at least one in all 12 rounds.

Richard Dent (203rd overall pick) sacks Dan Marino (27th overall pick) in a November 1991 game.

46 FOUR STRAIGHT SUPER BOWLS FOR BILLS

JANUARY 23, 1994

It's entirely accurate to say the Buffalo Bills are the only team ever to lose four straight Super Bowls. But isn't it kinder to say the Bills are the only team ever to play in the Super Bowl four years in a row? Because that, too, is accurate . . . and it's damn impressive. As years have gone by, their accomplishment has earned the gravitas it deserves. At the time, however, circumstances painted a sad picture.

The Bills were heavy favorites in their first Super Bowl appearance, but they lost to the Giants in Super Bowl XXV on a missed field goal in the closing seconds. A year later, they lost to the Redskins in a game that saw star running back Thurman Thomas miss the first two offensive snaps of the game because he couldn't find his helmet. They were outscored in the next two Super Bowls by the Dallas Cowboys, 82–30.

Maybe time will never heal all of those wounds, but it's hard not to appreciate the only team ever to win four straight conference title games. From that run, five players—quarterback Jim Kelly, running back Thurman Thomas, receivers Andre Reed and James Lofton, and defensive end Bruce Smith—are in the Pro Football Hall of Fame. So are head coach Marv Levy and general manager Bill Polian.

"It was such an example—if I'm looking for a positive in it—of the fantastic resiliency of the people on our team, in our organization," said Levy. "And really, our fans. They rallied around us. They greeted players with huge crowds when we came back from the game. That will always stick in my mind—the resilience of the players and the support from the fans."

The Bills' Super Bowl teams featured the fast-paced "K-Gun" offense that seemed to score at will. The defense, in addition to Smith, featured Pro Bowl linebackers Cornelius Bennett and Darryl Talley. Buffalo also had a not-so-secret weapon in Steve Tasker, widely regarded as the best special teams player in NFL history.

It was a very well-balanced team, gifted both physically and mentally.

"Very early in my tenure there, we were really determined to bring nothing but high-character players onto our team," said Levy. "Personalities might differ considerably, but did they show up for work? Not blame their teammates? Were good citizens? That was the most compelling reason, along with their pretty doggone good ability, why we were able to get back."

Despite the Super Bowl losses, there were plenty of high points for the Bills during their four-year run of excellence. From 1990 to '93, they were a combined 49–15 in the regular season and 9–4 in the postseason. The four AFC Championship Game victories came against four different teams. In 1990, they destroyed the Raiders, 51–3. In the next three AFC title games, they knocked off John Elway's Broncos, Dan Marino's Dolphins, and Joe Montana's Chiefs.

"It's something that I will always treasure," said Levy. "Sure, we would've wanted to win one—or all of them, for that matter—but you can't change it. It's just the fantastic resilience and character of those people."

47 SUPER BOWL HALFTIME BECOMES A SPECTACLE

JANUARY 31, 1993

Believe it or not, as recently as the early '90s, Super Bowl halftime shows were headlined by various college marching bands. That all changed at Super Bowl XXVII in Pasadena.

"We were quite literally into the dancing snowflakes era before that," said former NFL vice president of events Jim Steeg, who ran Super Bowl operations for the league from 1979 to 2004. The Super Bowl XXVI halftime show in Minnesota featured Olympic figure skaters Brian Boitano and Dorothy Hamill skating on ice in the middle of the Metrodome.

But what's more significant about the Super Bowl XXVI halftime show is that it was ambushed by FOX. The fledgling TV network was not yet an NFL broadcast partner at the time. FOX promoted a live episode of its hit sketch comedy show, *In Living Color*, which started just as the Super Bowl went to halftime and ended just as the CBS game broadcast came back from halftime.

"So it was alternative programming," said Steeg, noting that it did affect CBS' halftime ratings. "I think we consciously said, 'Okay, well, we've gotta do something about this.'"

So it was decided the NFL would book the biggest name they could possibly attract: Michael Jackson. The King of Pop electrified the Rose Bowl crowd. Jackson's performance is still one of the most watched halftime shows in Super Bowl history. More importantly, it was the moment that made Super Bowl halftime a "thing."

From that point on, the NFL went after big-name halftime acts every year.

"The irony is that to some degree that hurt us for a while, because when we approached other acts, they could not see themselves competing with it," said Steeg. Three years after Jackson, Diana Ross performed. Two years after that, it was Gloria Estefan and Stevie Wonder. The beginning of a steady run of superstars, however, didn't come until Super Bowl XXXVI, when U2 put on an inspiring show five months after 9/11.

Since then, the halftime show has featured the likes of Paul McCartney, the Rolling Stones, Prince, the Who, Bruce Springsteen, Beyonce, Bruno Mars, and Lady Gaga.

48

TAGLIABUE NAMED COMMISSIONER

OCTOBER 26, 1989

Replacing a legendary coach or player in the NFL has never been easy. Pete Rozelle was so successful in his role as commissioner of the NFL for 29 years that following him might have been akin to filling the shoes of Vince Lombardi or Dan Marino. Despite that pressure, Paul Tagliabue created an impactful legacy of his own.

Joe Browne, an NFL executive for 50 years who served under three commissioners (Rozelle, Tagliabue, and Roger Goodell), has long been a staunch supporter of the campaign to put Tagliabue into the Pro Football Hall of Fame.

"When Paul became commissioner in 1989, there was a general malaise in the league after the decade of the '80s consumed the owners and league office on negative matters such as defending needless litigation and two long player strikes," said Browne. "Paul quickly took charge and put his imprint on the league, most notably through negotiating on behalf of the owners a game-changing labor settlement in 1993 which gave players limited free agency and provided the clubs with a salary cap in order to ensure competitive balance."

In addition to his role in brokering labor peace, Tagliabue presided over the expansion of the league from 28 to 32 teams, implemented one of the strongest steroid policies in sports, and oversaw new stadium construction in communities across the league.

"There are singular issues alone that qualify him for enshrinement in Canton, including his work to keep the Saints in New Orleans after Hurricane Katrina and to help rebuild the entire business community there," said Browne.

Tagliabue also deserves much credit for his leadership in the days and months following the 9/11 terrorist attacks. And in 2002, he played a key role working with Pittsburgh Steelers owner Dan Rooney on the creation of the Rooney Rule.

101

49

THE *HEIDI* GAME

NOVEMBER 17, 1968

The New York Jets and Oakland Raiders were bitter rivals in the final days of the American Football League. They played several intense games in the late '60s, but their matchup on this particular date would go down in history as one of the most memorable regular-season games in AFL or NFL history.

Problem was, few people got to see the crazy ending.

That's because the game's broadcaster, NBC, was scheduled to air the children's movie *Heidi* starting at 7:00 PM Eastern time. NBC executives had actually made the decision that they would delay the start of the movie to show the game in its entirety. Problem is, the phone lines were tied up with viewers inquiring about the night's schedule. The execs couldn't get through to control. So at 7:00, viewers in the Eastern time zone were switched from the game to *Heidi*.

What did they miss? Only one of the more unlikely comebacks. Raiders quarterback Daryle Lamonica (seen here) had thrown a TD pass to Fred Biletnikoff to tie the game at 29 with less than four minutes left. But the Jets countered with a go-ahead field goal that made if 32–29 with a little over one minute left to play. On the ensuing drive—not seen by the East Coast fans—Lamonica found running back Charlie Smith for a 43-yard touchdown. Raiders, 36, Jets, 32. On the ensuing kickoff, the Jets fumbled and Oakland's Preston Ridlehuber returned it for a score that made the final 43–32.

Needless to say, fans were irate and there were ramifications. Going forward, NBC changed its communications system to ensure that executives would have a clear line to their control room to make last-minute decisions. And once the AFL and NFL were merged, the league mandated in its TV contracts that all games would be shown in their entirety in the visiting team's TV market.

As for the Raiders-Jets rivalry, they met again a month later in the AFL Championship Game, and the Jets avenged their loss in the *Heidi* Game. Two weeks later, they defeated the Baltimore Colts in Super Bowl III.

50

O.J. TOPS 2,000

DECEMBER 16, 1973

Future generations will have no idea that O.J. Simpson was once a beloved NFL superstar. Perhaps even today's younger generation only knows Simpson as an accused murderer who later served 10 years in prison for armed robbery and kidnapping. Not to detract from the severity of those offenses, but it's also worth noting here that Simpson is responsible for perhaps the greatest single season an NFL running back has ever had.

After winning the 1968 Heisman Trophy at USC, Simpson played the first nine of his 11 NFL seasons with the Buffalo Bills. He led the league with 1,251 rushing yards in 1972, but that was a mere tease of what was to come.

Simpson opened the 1973 season with 250 yards at New England. With dazzling speed and the ability to cut and change direction without slowing, Simpson continued to carve his way through the league. Only three times did he fail to rush for at least 100 yards. In Week 13, Simpson gashed the Patriots again, this time for 219 yards. With one game left in the 14-week season, Simpson had 1,803 yards. The single-season rushing record was 1,863, which was set in 1963 by the immortal Jim Brown. No player had come within 200 yards of Brown's record until now.

Getting 61 yards to break the record would not be easy. Simpson and the Bills ended the season against the New York Jets at Shea Stadium, and the game was played in a snowstorm.

Then again, what's a little snow to a team from Buffalo? Running behind an offensive line nicknamed "The Electric Company," Simpson smashed Brown's record. He rushed for 200 yards to finish the season with an NFL-record 2,003 yards.

Simpson remains the only player in NFL history to rush for 2,000 yards in a 14-game season. Only six players (Eric Dickerson, Barry Sanders, Terrell Davis, Jamal Lewis, Chris Johnson, and Adrian Peterson) have topped 2,000 yards since, all in 16 games.

A Chicago Bears receiver goes up to make a catch in an early NFL game, circa 1920s.

Odell Beckham Jr. makes a one-handed catch for a touchdown against the Dallas Cowboys in a November 2014 game.

51

CRAZYLEGS SMASHES RECEIVING RECORD

1951

Before there was Jerry Rice and Calvin Johnson, there was Elroy "Crazylegs" Hirsch. Even though the NFL blossomed in the 1950s into a league where passing became the dominant form of offense, it would still be decades before fans saw the kind of eye-popping numbers that wide receivers have now made routine. Which is what makes Hirsch's 1951 season all the more fantastic.

Elroy "Crazylegs" Hirsch of the Los Angeles Rams set a new single-season NFL record that year with 1,495 receiving yards, and he helped the Rams win the 1951 NFL championship. Technically, the record stood for 33 years. Two receivers had higher totals in the 1960s playing in the more pass-happy American Football League—Charley Hennigan did it in 1961 and '64 for the Houston Oilers and Lance Alworth did it in 1964 for the San Diego Chargers—but no player on an NFL team topped Crazylegs' number until Roy Green had 1,555 yards for the St. Louis Cardinals in 1984.

Hirsch's record was a full 284 yards more than the previous NFL record at the time, Don Hutson's 1,211 yards in 1942. Amazingly, it was the only 1,000-yard season of Hirsch's NFL career. In nine seasons, all with the Rams, Hirsch caught 343 passes for 6,299 yards and 53 touchdowns. He was elected to the Pro Football Hall of Fame in 1967.

52

SEA OF HANDS

DECEMBER 21, 1974

The Oakland Raiders played many games that were big enough to earn special names—like the "Holy Roller" and "Ghost to the Post." But the "Sea of Hands" game was probably the most impactful of the bunch.

In an AFC playoff game against the two-time defending champion Miami Dolphins, Kenny "the Snake" Stabler threw a game-winning eight-yard touchdown pass to running back Clarence Davis, who somehow came down with the ball in the middle of a swarm of defenders.

"That was big, because that gave us a chance to move onto the next round against the Steelers, and the guy with the worst hands on our offense ends up catching the touchdown between three or four guys," laughed Raiders Hall of Fame left tackle Art Shell. "Clarence Davis had the worst hands of all the running backs and receivers."

Shell remembers the play well—it was a play the Raiders called often when they were near the goal line, and with great success.

"Fake bootleg," says Shell. "Snake has the option of throwing the pass or running with it. [Hall of Fame guard] Gene [Upshaw] would pull out and lead. But somebody got hold of Snake's leg and he was getting ready to go down. And he just threw it up and Clarence ended up coming up with that ball. I don't know how he did it, but it was a big catch for us."

53 THE DRIVE

JANUARY 11, 1987

Having just scored to take a 20–13 lead in the AFC Championship Game, the Cleveland Browns were 5:32 from going to their first Super Bowl. With the Denver Broncos starting the ensuing drive on their own 2-yard line, all Cleveland had to do was prevent John Elway from driving his team 98 yards down the field. Well . . .

This would be Elway's first shining moment. In 1986, his fourth season in the league, Elway earned the first of his nine career Pro Bowl nods, leading the Broncos to an 11–5 record and AFC West crown. The Browns, led by head coach Marty Schottenheimer, finished the season with the AFC's best record, 12–4.

Elway brought his team to the line of scrimmage at the 2-yard line and completed a five-yard pass to running back Sammy Winder on first down—the start of

what would be a 15-play drive. Denver had reached the Cleveland 40-yard line with 1:52 left when Elway was sacked by Dave Puzzuoli, forcing a third-and-18. Elway responded with a 20-yard completion to Mark Jackson. Finally, on third-and-1 from the Cleveland 5-yard line, Elway found Jackson again, this time for the game-tying touchdown.

The momentum of "The Drive" rendered overtime a moot point. On Denver's first possession in OT, Elway led Denver on a nine-play, 60-yard drive that resulted in Rich Karlis' game-winning 33-yard field goal.

Two weeks later, Elway made the first of his five Super Bowl appearances with the Broncos. They lost in Super Bowl XXI to the New York Giants, but that did little to take away from the magic of "The Drive."

Arthur Sampson and William A. Shea
(Boston Yankees)

Charles Bidwill
(Chicago Cardinals)

Arthur J. Rooney
(Pittsburgh Steelers)

Curly Lambeau
(Green Bay Packers)

George Hala
(Chicago Bea

54 BELL NAMED COMMISSIONER

JANUARY 11, 1946

Bert Bell had been a co-founder and owner of the Philadelphia Eagles (1933–40) and then co-owner of the Pittsburgh Steelers (1940–45) before replacing Elmer Layden as commissioner of the NFL. Among other things, Bell played a major role in creating parity in the NFL—decades before that term was used to describe the league.

Even before he became commissioner, Bell played a key role in the NFL adopting the draft in 1936, ensuring that teams with the worst records got the highest picks to help them compete. Once named commissioner, one of Bell's first moves was to take over the schedule-making process. Always a hotly contested subject among owners before, Bell made a point to schedule evenly

Bert Bell (commissioner)

George Marshall
(Washington Redskins)

John V. Mara
(New York Giants)

Charles Walsh
(L.A. Rams)

Gus Dorias
(Detroit Lions)

Harry Thayer
(Philadelphia Eagles)

matched games at the beginning of the season with the intention of having as many teams as possible in contention for the title by season's end.

The beginning of Bell's tenure was highlighted by his decision to allow the Cleveland Rams to relocate to Los Angeles—which also precipitated the breaking of the color barrier when the Rams signed African American players Kenny Washington and Woody Strode.

By the end of Bell's tenure, the NFL's popularity was growing fast thanks to more games being televised.

55 FIRST TV MEGADEAL

APRIL 17, 1964

Three years into Pete Rozelle's tenure as commissioner, the league's marketing was such that the NFL was becoming a valuable TV product. On the heels of the 1958 title game, CBS had paid about $5 million for the rights to broadcast NFL games in 1963. That number was about to balloon.

In January of 1964, Rozelle advised the big three broadcast networks—CBS, NBC, and ABC—that the league would hold open bidding for a two-year TV package. The plan was for the networks to submit sealed bids. According to the industry legend, the deck may have been stacked in the incumbent's favor.

Reportedly, there was a mole at ABC who leaked that network's bid to the NFL. And according to CBS broadcasting legend Pat Summerall, Rozelle called CBS executive Bill MacPhail before the bids were submitted and told him NBC's bid was higher than theirs. Rozelle said CBS had to up their bid because he didn't want NBC getting the package.

All three networks' bids were much higher than what CBS had paid the year before, with CBS on top. The winning bid: $28.2 million for two years. They paid an additional $1.8 million apiece for the 1964 and '65 championship games.

Some at the NFL thought the triumphant TV deal would also strike a blow against the upstart American Football League, but that was not the case. Not long after CBS got the NFL package, NBC locked up a five-year, $36 million deal with the AFL. That package was just as important as the NFL-CBS deal, as it ensured the AFL would stick around long enough to give the NFL a run for its money.

Dan Currie, Ray Nitschke, and Willie Davis of the Packers sit on the bench during a December 1960 victory against the 49ers.

56

THE COMEBACK: BILLS-OILERS

JANUARY 3, 1993

Pro Football Hall of Famer Warren Moon is one of the best NFL quarterbacks who never played in the Super Bowl. The 1992 season may have been his best chance to get there—especially when his Houston Oilers had a 32-point lead in the third quarter of this AFC play-off game against the Buffalo Bills.

The Bills had nothing to lose. The two-time defending AFC champions were without future Hall of Fame quarterback Jim Kelly, so they just let loose with super-sub Frank Reich. Reich had already notched the greatest comeback in college football history when he was at the University of Maryland. Why not match that feat in the pros?

Sure enough, Reich led Buffalo on a furious comeback. The Bills actually took a 38–35 lead and the Oilers had to come back themselves to tie it late in the game to force overtime. When Nate Odomes intercepted Moon in overtime, it set up Steve Christie's game-winning field goal. Final: Bills 41, Oilers 38.

"Naturally, when you're down by as much as we were, you just hope that you score a couple of times and make it respectable," Bills owner Ralph Wilson said after the game. "You never expect a team to come back like ours did. Anybody who does is dreaming."

It was, as it turned out, a nightmare for the Oilers. Reich threw four second-half TD passes, three to future Hall of Fame receiver Andre Reed.

Amazingly, the Bills' stunning comeback was just the Wild Card game in that season's playoff run. Six days later, the Bills had to travel to Pittsburgh, where they defeated the Steelers. A week after that, they were on the road to face Dan Marino and the Miami Dolphins in the AFC title game. That win earned Buffalo its third consecutive trip to the Super Bowl. It was the third of an NFL-record four straight Super Bowl appearances—unfortunately for the Bills, all losses.

57

1998 NFL DRAFT: MANNING OR LEAF

APRIL 18, 1998

By all accounts, the question of who would be the number one overall pick in the 1998 NFL Draft was a toss-up. Would it be Peyton Manning, everyone's All-American who had just completed four stellar seasons at the University of Tennessee? Or would it be Ryan Leaf, the rifle-armed quarterback who threw 34 touchdown passes in 1997 and led Washington State to its first-ever Pac-10 title?

Despite how utterly different their NFL careers turned out, it really could have gone either way.

"Manning had a lesser arm, was not as fast, but he was probably the hardest-working guy you'd ever be around, fabulous work habits, great accuracy," said Gil Brandt, the former Cowboys personnel director who was an NFL.com draft guru when the '98 Draft took place. Brandt is convinced that Colts general manager Bill Polian was undecided on the pick until late in the process.

"I do think there was a 50-50 chance the Colts could have taken Leaf," Brandt said. "Polian said there was never any doubt in his mind. We don't know that and never will."

The Colts made Manning the top pick, and the rest is history. Manning finished his 18-year career with 71,940 passing yards, 539 touchdowns, and two Super Bowl victories. Leaf, meanwhile, lasted just three seasons in the league, causing trouble both on and off the field.

The San Diego Chargers had actually traded up from third to second in the first round of the draft, figuring that they would be happy with whichever of the two quarterbacks the Colts didn't take. So when Polian selected Manning, San Diego general manager Bobby Beathard pulled the trigger on Leaf. It was a decision the team would regret, as Leaf's bad attitude and sense of entitlement made him the complete opposite of Manning when it came to leadership. His career was stymied by injuries, bad behavior, and poor play.

"Guys can be jerks, but I've never seen a guy that worked harder at alienating his teammates," Beathard once said.

The Manning-Leaf draft might be one of the all-time great "what if" debates in NFL history. What if the Colts drafted Leaf instead of Manning? Would Manning have led the Chargers to a Super Bowl? And if Leaf struggled in Indianapolis the way he did in San Diego, maybe the Colts would have been in position to draft Philip Rivers six years later. Or perhaps they'd have chosen Eli Manning.

58

DAN MARINO'S RECORD-BREAKING SEASON

1984

Of the six quarterbacks selected in the first round of the 1983 NFL Draft, Dan Marino was the last to hear his name called. In just his second year with the Miami Dolphins, however, he became the first of the group to reach the Super Bowl after producing one of the greatest seasons an NFL quarterback has ever had.

A less than spectacular senior season at the University of Pittsburgh and some rumors of recreational drug use hurt Marino's draft status. The Miami Dolphins drafted him with the 27th overall pick—second-to-last in Round 1. Dolphins legendary head coach Don Shula has acknowledged that Marino was highly motivated to make his mark in the NFL to make teams regret their decision to pass on him.

And it did not take long for that to happen. Marino became Miami's starting QB midway through his rookie season and made the Pro Bowl after throwing 20 touchdown passes against just six interceptions. Dolphins fans were excited about the prospects for their new franchise quarterback, but they could not have imagined the kind of numbers Marino was about to produce in just his second NFL season.

With his canon arm and a lightning-quick release, Marino confounded pass rushers who rarely got to him before he could find his intended target. In 1984, Marino dropped back to pass 564 times and was sacked just 13 times. When the dust cleared on his incredible season, Marino had obliterated the single-season records for passing yards and touchdowns. He was the first quarterback to break the 5,000-yard plateau (5,084) and his 48 TD passes were 12 more than the previous record, which had stood for 23 years.

Marino's season yardage record stood for 27 years, until Drew Brees broke it in 2011. Only Brees, Tom Brady, Peyton Manning, Ben Roethlisberger, and Patrick Mahomes have passed for more yards in a season. Marino's 48 TD passes were the standard for 20 years, until Manning had 49 in 2004. Manning set another record with 55 in 2013, and only Manning, Brady, and Patrick Mahomes have had more than 48 TD passes in a season since Marino's 1984 campaign.

After Marino's record-setting regular season, he set an AFC Championship Game record with 421 yards in a win over the Pittsburgh Steelers. He passed for 318 yards in Super Bowl XIX but was on the losing end of that game to Joe Montana and the 49ers.

Few would have believed at that time that Marino would never get back to the Super Bowl, yet that was the case. When he retired in 1999, he held the career marks for passing yards and touchdowns, records that have since been broken, and he was inducted into the Pro Football Hall of Fame in 2005.

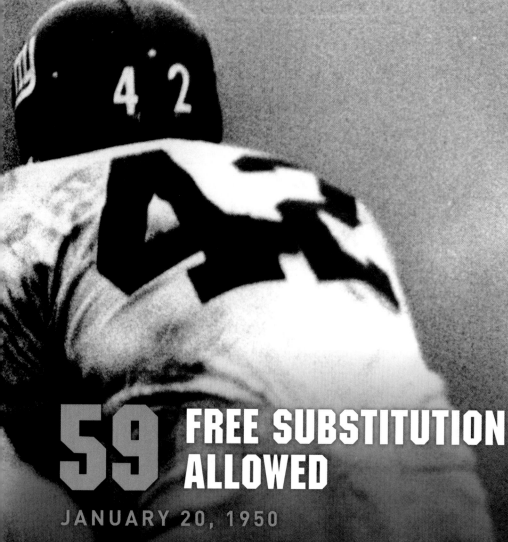

59 FREE SUBSTITUTION ALLOWED

JANUARY 20, 1950

In today's NFL, we have nickel packages, dime packages, third-down specialists, and even "Wildcat" quarterbacks. It's likely we'd have none of that if not for the rule change in 1950 that allowed for unlimited substitution.

Before 1949, the NFL had a rule stating that teams could not substitute more than three players at a time. During the '49 season, the league experimented with unlimited free substitution—and made it an official rule in 1950. Not only did this open the door for specialization, it cleared the way for the two-platoon era.

Let's face it, limiting players to just offense or just defense is really the most basic form of specialization. And it had an immediate impact on the game. As football historian Sean Lehman wrote in *The Football Abstract*:

"For the NFL's first three decades, versatility was the most important trait for a player. Your starting quarterback had to be quick enough to play safety, your running backs tough enough to play linebacker. The downside to this approach was that a player with one specific skill—say blazing speed—might not be enough of an all-around player to crack the starting lineup. With free substitution legalized, specialization became the norm . . .. Free substitution helped the passing game immensely because it allowed coaches to use quick players at offensive end who weren't big enough to play defense. Their speed could be used as a weapon, and many teams moved to formations that featured three ends and just two backs."

Chuck Bednarik: the last two-way man.

CHIEFS-DOLPHINS' DOUBLE OT

DECEMBER 25, 1971

The 1971 divisional playoff game between the Miami Dolphins and Kansas City Chiefs on Christmas Day only *seemed* as if it went on until New Year's. According to the game clock, it really lasted 82 minutes and 40 seconds. Still, that was enough to make it the longest NFL game ever played.

Miami won, 27–24, when Garo Yepremian kicked a 37-yard field goal 7:40 into the second overtime period.

The game was much more than a marathon contest. It was a back-and-forth affair. The fact that it was a

playoff game, on Christmas Day, with Hall of Famers up and down the field, makes it not only the longest game ever played, but one of the *greatest* games ever played.

The Dolphins featured six future Hall of Famers on their roster, coached by Hall of Famer Don Shula. The Chiefs had seven Hall of Fame players and Hall of Fame coach Hank Stram.

Kansas City jumped out to a 10–0 lead in the first quarter, but Miami came back to tie the game at 10 by halftime. At the end of the third quarter, the game

was tied at 17. Kansas City took a 24–17 lead in the fourth, only to have Miami tie it again with 1:25 left in regulation.

Ed Podolak then returned the ensuing kickoff 78 yards, putting the Chiefs in position to win. But at the 15-yard line with 35 seconds left, Hall of Fame kicker Jan Stenerud missed what would have been the game-winning field goal.

In the first overtime, Stenerud had a 42-yard field goal blocked and Yepremian missed a 52-yard try.

Finally, midway through the second overtime, Yepremian kicked the game-winner.

"It seemed like we played three games that day," said Chiefs Hall of Fame linebacker Bobby Bell. "Once you get to the fourth quarter, you've already played your heart out. Then the next thing you know they say you're playing overtime. And that's another game in itself. Then we had to play again . . . It was one of the toughest games I ever played in."

SUPER BOWL SHUFFLE

DECEMBER 3, 1985

ow good were the 1985 Chicago Bears? Well, they were one of the best teams in NFL history . . . and they knew it.

The Bears were so sure of themselves that they e a music video—"The Super Bowl Shuffle"—and ased it two months before Super Bowl XX was ever ed. You can debate their place among the best s of all-time, but one thing is undeniable: the '85 s were the cockiest NFL champs of all time.

And what a cast of characters it was. The record-set- defense, which swore its allegiance to defensive

coordinator Buddy Ryan, featured three future Hall of Famers in defensive tackle Dan Hampton, defensive end Richard Dent, and middle linebacker Mike Singletary. Rookie defensive tackle William "Refrigerator" Perry took the league by storm and became a fan favorite—partially for his defense but more for his occasional appearances as a 335-pound short-yardage back. The offense featured the "punky QB," Jim McMahon, and Hall of Fame running back Walter Payton. "Sweetness" was nearing the end of his career but was still a dangerous offensive threat.

Of course, they all took their marching orders from head coach Mike Ditka, whose brash attitude embodied the city of Chicago.

The Bears absolutely steamrolled through the play-offs, and their defense ruled throughout. They didn't allow a single point in getting to the Super Bowl, out-scoring the New York Giants and Los Angeles Rams by a combined score of 45–0. In the AFC, the New England Patriots defeated Miami to earn a spot in Super Bowl XX. It was the first Super Bowl in franchise history for the Patriots.

They never had a chance.

Patriots quarterback Tony Eason was pummeled by the Bears defense and Chicago cruised to a 46–10 win. Ditka and Ryan were both carried off by their players. The only negative for the Bears was that many fans were critical of Ditka for letting the Fridge score on a one-yard plunge instead of giving the beloved Payton his chance to score a touchdown in the Super Bowl.

Perhaps that move created some bad karma. That's one of the only reasons to explain why a team that was so dominant in 1985 never got back to the Super Bowl.

62 NEW CBA OPENS DOOR FOR MODERN-DAY FREE AGENCY

1993

The NFL had a simple form of free agency dating back to 1947, but for the most part it was very restrictive. In the '60s, Pete Rozelle instituted a rule that stated if a team signed a free agent, it had to provide compensation to the player's former team. In most cases, the compensation wasn't worth it.

As players got more fed up with their limited options in the 1970s and '80s, they unionized and started pushing for more rights. Recognizing they needed to do something, league officials in 1989 introduced "Plan B" free agency. Under the Plan B system, teams could protect up to 37 players on their roster, with the remaining players not under contract free to sign elsewhere.

As you can imagine, the best players were protected; Plan B failed to produce any significant player movement. The players union disbanded, allowing for individual players to sue the NFL. In 1992, a federal court ruled that Plan B violated ant-trust laws.

With Plan B done, then-commissioner Paul Tagliabue and NFLPA director Gene Upshaw brokered a new collective bargaining agreement that paved the way for true free agency. The compromise that allowed owners to agree to the deal was the implementation of the franchise tag, allowing them to protect their best players, and the salary cap, to ensure that payrolls don't get completely out of control.

The first salary cap, in 1994, was $34.6 million per team; in 2019, the cap was $188.2 million.

While there have been tweaks to the system and the numbers have grown as the overall business has grown, the free agency system that took shape in 1993 has withstood the test of time and shaped the way the NFL looks today.

Marcus Allen: one of the first major free agents.

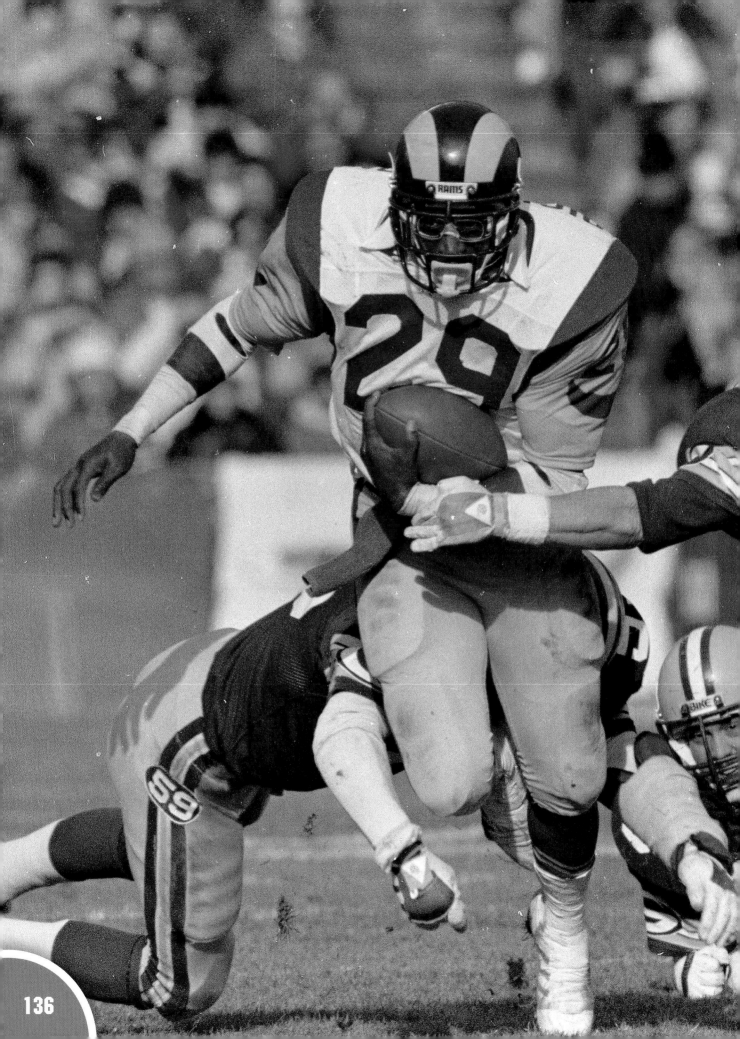

63 ERIC DICKERSON'S RECORD-BREAKING SEASON

1984

To say that Eric Dickerson set the bar high in his first season in the NFL is an understatement. Dickerson, the second overall pick in the stellar 1983 Draft, had a rookie season for the ages: the Los Angeles Rams tailback set rookie records with 1,808 rushing yards and 18 rushing touchdowns—both records still stand today.

What would he do for an encore? How about shatter the NFL single-season rushing record . . .

Dickerson rushed for 138 yards in the 1984 season opener against Dallas. That would be the first of a record 12 100-yard games that season. In the mix was a 208-yard effort in Week 10 against the Cardinals and 191 yards in Week 13 at Tampa Bay. After he rushed for 215 yards in Week 15 against the Houston Oilers, Dickerson was at 2,007 yards for the season—joining O.J. Simpson

as the only 2,000-yard rushers in NFL history and breaking Simpson's mark of 2,003. One week later, Dickerson finished his record-breaking season with a total of 2,105 yards.

Six players have topped 2,000 yards since then, but none has bested Dickerson's mark.

In four full seasons with the Rams, Dickerson averaged an incredible 1,742 yards per season. But a contract dispute led the Rams to trade him to the Indianapolis Colts in a blockbuster deal three games into the 1987 season. Dickerson had three 1,000-yard seasons with the Colts before injuries began to take a toll. When he retired in 1993, his career rushing total of 13,259 yards was second to Walter Payton.

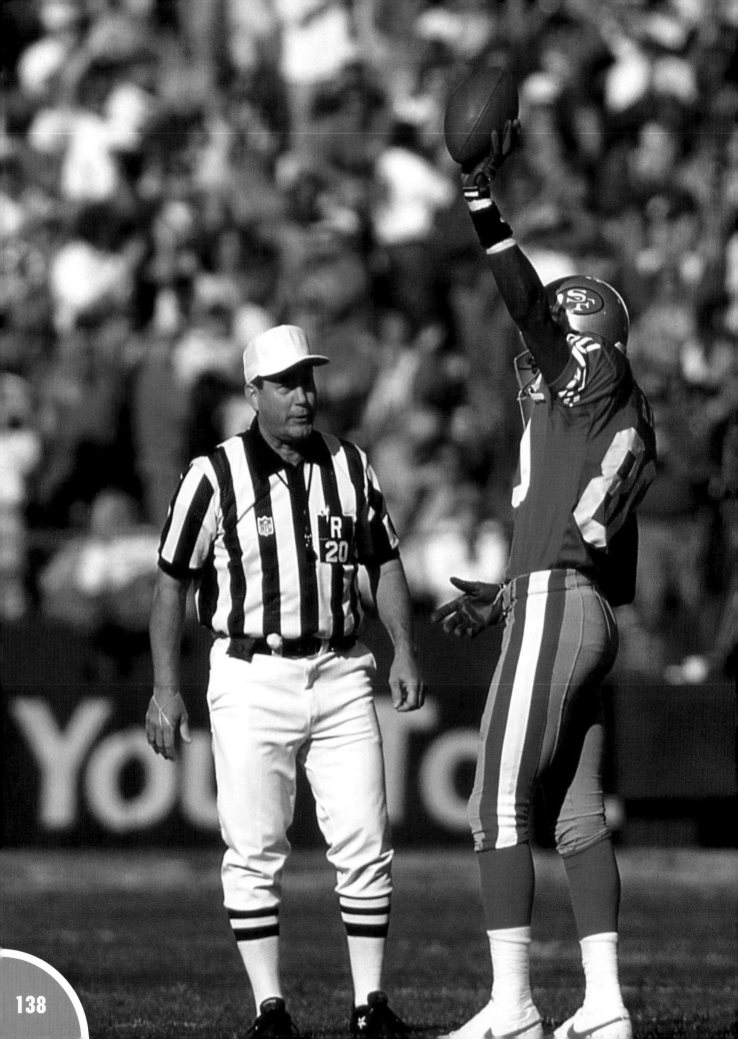

64

JERRY RICE'S RECORD-BREAKING SEASON

1995

Jerry Rice wasn't the fastest wide receiver when he came out of Mississippi Valley State, which is why he was still on the board midway through the 1985 NFL Draft. The Dallas Cowboys, who had the 17th overall pick, were interested in Rice . . . but so was San Francisco 49ers head coach Bill Walsh. Coming off a win in Super Bowl XIX, the 49ers had the last pick in Round 1, so when the New England Patriots went on the clock with the 16th pick, Walsh offered them their first- and second-round picks to move up. Thus, Jerry Rice was a 49er.

Amazingly, Rice had been in the league for 10 years and was the MVP of Super Bowl XXIII before he enjoyed his greatest single season. In 1995, Rice set career highs with 122 receptions for 1,848 yards.

In a career that lasted 20 years, Rice was consistently outstanding, to the point that many consider him the greatest player in NFL history regardless of position. The numbers speak for themselves. Rice played in an era when a plethora of standout receivers posted Hall of Fame–caliber statistics—yet Rice's career marks are still out of reach.

Rice's 1,549 career receptions are 224 more than second-place holder Tony Gonzalez.

His 22,895 receiving yards are 6,616 more than the total for Larry Fitzgerald, who entered 2019 in second place.

It's fairly safe to say his record of 197 touchdown receptions will never be in danger. Randy Moss is currently second on that list with 156.

65

"THIS ONE'S FOR JOHN"

JANUARY 25, 1998

By 1997, it looked as if John Elway was destined to go down in NFL history as one of the greatest quarterbacks who never won a Super Bowl. To make matters worse, he had actually been to three Super Bowls but came up short all three times. Entering his 15th season, the 37-year-old Elway was running out of chances.

Even when Denver made it to Super Bowl XXXII in San Diego, Elway faced an uphill battle. The AFC had lost 13 straight Super Bowls, Elway's three losses among them. Denver's opponent in this game, the defending champion Green Bay Packers, arrived in San Diego as an 11-point favorite.

But the Broncos rose to the challenge and led for much of the game. Elway didn't throw a touchdown pass in the game, but he had two very important runs. The first was a one-yard TD run early in the second quarter to give Denver a 14–7 lead. Then, with the score tied at 17 in the third quarter, Denver faced a third-and-6 at the Green Bay 12-yard line. Elway ended up scrambling

eight yards for the first down—being hit by two Packers defenders at the end of the run and spinning like a helicopter before crashing to the turf. Two plays later, Terrell Davis scored on a 1-yard run to put the Broncos up, 24–17.

Two minutes into the fourth quarter, a Brett Favre TD pass tied the game at 24. The game remained tied until Davis scored his third touchdown of the game with 1:45 left to play—to give Denver a 31–24 lead that would become the final score.

Davis, who rushed for 157 yards and those three scores—despite missing a good chunk of the second quarter with a migraine—was the game's MVP. Elway only passed for 123 yards in the game, with no touchdowns and one interception, but there was no question that the storyline of the game was this future Hall of Famer getting the monkey off his back.

Broncos owner Pat Bowlen raised the Vince Lombardi Trophy during the televised postgame celebration and declared: "This one's for John!"

66 BARRY SANDERS RETIRES

JULY 28, 1999

Like another all-time great running back before him, Detroit Lions star Barry Sanders stunned the football world by retiring from the game when he seemingly had several productive seasons in him. It was reminiscent of Cleveland Browns legend Jim Brown, who retired at the age of 30 after just nine NFL seasons. Their styles were different but the results were similar. Sanders, so quick and explosive on the football field, was 31 when he retired. He averaged 1,388 rushing yards per season. He had just rushed for 1,491 yards in 1998—and he needed just 1,457 more yards at the time to pass Walter Payton for the NFL's career mark (a record since broken by Emmitt Smith).

Some speculated that Sanders stepped away because he was unhappy with the Lions' efforts to field the best team possible. Some wondered if Sanders—who seemed shy and uncomfortable in the spotlight—wasn't eager to take the all-time rushing crown away from a figure as beloved as Payton.

"I think he just felt like it was time," said Bobby Ross, Detroit's head coach from 1997 to 2000. When Sanders announced his retirement, he simply said in a statement that his desire to leave the game was greater than his desire to play.

While the desire might have diminished, the talent never wavered. Which makes you wonder how incredible Sanders' numbers could have been had he played just a few more years.

Over the last five years of his career, Sanders averaged 100 yards per game. If he maintained that level for three more seasons, he would have finished with 20,000 yards—1,645 yards more than Smith's current all-time mark.

"I've never experienced a player more than Barry with the idea in mind that he's gonna score every time he touches the ball," said Ross.

67

SUPER BOWL XXXIV: ONE YARD SHORT

JANUARY 30, 2000

For the first three decades of the Super Bowl era, a majority of the NFL's championship games had one thing in common: They weren't very close. Of the first 33 Super Bowls, 24 were decided by 10 or more points.

The closest Super Bowl played in the 20th century was XXV, when the Giants beat the Bills, 20–19, after Scott Norwood missed a last-minute field goal. The first title game played in this century wasn't as close based on point differential, but it was the first Super Bowl that was truly in doubt until the very last play of the game.

The St. Louis Rams won their first Super Bowl, 23–16, when Tennessee Titans wide receiver Kevin Dyson was tackled at the 1-yard line as time expired. Ironically, it was Dyson who scored the "Music City Miracle" touchdown just a few weeks earlier to beat Buffalo and help the Titans advance in the AFC playoffs.

The Rams took a 23–16 lead thanks to a 73-yard touchdown pass from Kurt Warner to Isaac Bruce with just 1:54 left to play. Titans quarterback Steve McNair led Tennessee on a potential game-tying drive—reaching the St. Louis 10-yard line with six seconds on the clock. McNair hit Dyson about two-and-a-half yards shy of the

goal line. Dyson desperately reached for the end zone as Rams linebacker Mike Jones wrapped up Dyson's legs and made the tackle. When Dyson went down, he was mere inches from the goal line. Game over.

That play capped one of the truly remarkable seasons for one player in NFL history. When the 1999 season began, the Rams had brought in free agent Trent Green to be their new starting quarterback, but Green promptly suffered a season-ending knee injury in training camp. Warner, a former Arena League quarterback, was only on the roster because the Cleveland Browns didn't select him when he was left unprotected for the expansion draft. Rams head coach Dick Vermeil gave Warner the starting job and the expectations around the league could not have been lower. But Warner rose to the occasion and went from no-name to superstar in a flash. Leading the Rams' "Greatest Show on Turf" offense, Warner passed for 4,353 yards and 41 touchdowns in 1999. In Super Bowl XXXIV, he passed for 414 yards and two touchdowns—becoming the sixth player in NFL history to be named MVP in both the regular season and the Super Bowl.

68

NFL VS. USFL

JULY 29, 1986

The United States Football League began in 1983 with a combination of former NFL veterans and big-name rookies. Created as a spring league, the on-field product was an early success, featuring future NFL stars such as Jim Kelly, Steve Young, Herschel Walker, and Reggie White. But the USFL leadership may have been too aggressive for its own good. After just one season, they expanded from 12 to 18 teams. At the conclusion of their third season, in 1985, they announced that the 1986 season would be played in the fall—going head-to-head with the NFL.

Several USFL teams folded after the 1985 season, and the league encountered too many obstacles to continue. They ceased operations before the '86 season began—instead filing a $1.7 billion dollar antitrust lawsuit against the NFL. The USFL contended the NFL had a monopoly, making it difficult for another league to secure TV rights or stadium venues.

"When they realized their self-inflicted mistakes, they moved to Plan B and sued the NFL," recalled Joe Browne, an NFL executive at the time. "However, a federal jury in New York quickly realized the USFL's downfall was no one's fault but its own and ruled against the new league on all the major charges that they had brought into the courtroom."

Technically, the USFL won the lawsuit, though it was hardly a victory. The jury agreed the NFL was a monopoly, but it also concluded that the NFL did not impede the USFL's efforts and that the USFL was pushing to create a merger with the NFL.

Instead of the $1.7 billion the USFL was seeking, the jury awarded them one dollar. Under antitrust rules, the award was tripled to three dollars.

"Moral of the story is that a new league must walk before it runs," said Browne, "and the league operators need to be business-savvy and have deep financial pockets."

Kelvin Bryant hoists the USFL championship trophy. ➤

Deion Sanders and Jerry Rice go at
it in a 1995 game in Dallas.

69

SUPER BOWL XXII: DOUG WILLIAMS

JANUARY 31, 1988

When the 1987 season began, there was really no reason to imagine that Doug Williams might become the first African American quarterback to start in a Super Bowl. Williams, who was in his seventh NFL season, was the Washington Redskins' backup for most of the year. But starting QB Jay Schroeder was injured and inefficient for much of the season, and so head coach Joe Gibbs tabbed Williams to be his starter in the postseason. And after playoff wins over the Bears and Vikings, Williams and the Redskins had a date with the Denver Broncos in Super Bowl XXII in San Diego.

Once there, however, it looked like Williams' historic moment might be a footnote. The Broncos, making their second straight Super Bowl appearance with John Elway at the helm, jumped out to a 10–0 lead after the first quarter of play.

Then the floodgates opened.

With Williams leading the way, the Redskins exploded for a Super Bowl–record 35 points in the second quarter. By halftime, Williams had four touchdown passes—a Super Bowl record for one half, let alone one quarter.

When Washington scored its final touchdown in the fourth quarter, they had tallied 42 unanswered points after trailing 10–0. Williams finished with 340 yards passing and those four TD strikes. In addition to becoming the first African American quarterback to win an NFL championship of any kind, he was also named Super Bowl XXII MVP.

70

RAIDERS VS. THE NFL

MAY 7, 1982

When it comes to head-to-head matchups, the Raiders have a career record of 1–1 . . . against the league office.

Oakland Raiders owner Al Davis had a contentious relationship with the NFL and commissioner Pete Rozelle, some people saying it dated back to the AFL-NFL merger. Davis was commissioner of the AFL at the time, but he was kept out of the secret merger talks.

More relevant, though, was the fact that by the end of the 1970s, Davis wanted to move the Raiders from Oakland to Los Angeles—a move that the NFL blocked in 1980. Davis and the Raiders filed an anti-trust lawsuit against the NFL . . . which made things pretty awkward at the end of the 1980 season.

Still in Oakland, the Raiders won the AFC title. After they defeated the Philadelphia Eagles in Super Bowl XV, Rozelle had to hand the Lombardi Trophy to Davis. Rozelle held the trophy with two hands when he passed it to Davis—some speculated that was a strategy to avoid the possibility that Davis would not shake his hand.

Two years later, a federal district court ruled in favor of the Raiders, and the team began playing in Los Angeles in 1982. A year later, the Raiders won Super Bowl XVIII. Again, Rozelle had to hand Davis the Lombardi Trophy.

The Raiders moved back to Oakland in 1995, after which the Raiders sued the NFL again. Davis claimed that the league sabotaged his efforts to get a new stadium deal in the Los Angeles area. This time, the league won.

71 PHILLY SPECIAL
FEBRUARY 4, 2018

It was Week 14 of the 2017 season when Philadelphia Eagles quarterback Carson Wentz went down with a season-ending knee injury. For Eagles fans, a calamity. Wentz to that point was an MVP candidate and the team was enjoying its finest season in years. With backup Nick Foles forced into action, Philadelphia fans that were raised to expect the worst had no reason to think this would finally be their year.

Foles stepped in and helped the Eagles beat the Falcons and Vikings in the playoffs, setting up a meeting with the New England Patriots in Super Bowl LII at Minnesota's U.S. Bank Stadium.

The Eagles were up 15–12 in the second quarter, and were in position to add to the lead just before halftime. Facing a fourth-and-goal at the New England 1-yard line with under a minute in the half, Eagles head coach Doug Pederson made the decision to go for it.

The play of the game to that point quickly became one of the most memorable plays in Super Bowl history.

Foles lined up in the shotgun, but then moved off to the right. Running back Corey Clement took the direct snap and pitched the ball to tight end Trey Burton. Rolling to his right, Burton tossed the ball to Foles, who was wide open in the end zone, for the stunning score.

The play—known as the Philly Special—gave the Eagles a 22–12 halftime lead. Somewhat overshadowed by the Philly Special is the fact that New England fought its way back and actually took a 33–32 lead midway through the fourth quarter.

Foles, who had the game of his life, led the Eagles on a 75-yard drive, including a fourth-and-1 conversion from their own 45, and threw the go-ahead touchdown pass to Zach Ertz with 2:21 left to play. The Eagles iced the game with a field goal and took home the Lombardi Trophy with a 41–33 victory.

72

PETE GOGOLAK POACHED BY GIANTS

MAY 17, 1966

Placekicker Pete Gogolak had a profound impact on pro football for two completely different reasons.

For starters, when he was drafted and signed by the Buffalo Bills of the American Football League in 1964, he became the first soccer-style kicker in pro football.

Two years later, he really made history, when he left the Bills and signed a contract with the NFL's New York Giants.

While there had always been stiff competition between the rival leagues for draft picks, there was an unwritten rule that the leagues would not "poach" players that were already on rosters. The Gogolak signing, however, ratcheted up the hostility between the two leagues. The bad news was that poaching became a problem.

The good news was that this escalated feud led to the merger. As a direct result of the Gogolak signing, Oakland Raiders co-owner Al Davis took over as AFL commissioner and encouraged the signing of NFL stars such as John Brodie, Mike Ditka, and Roman Gabriel.

Within a month, however, the merger was in place.

73 COLTS LEAVE BALTIMORE

MARCH 28, 1984

The Colts franchise had been a fixture in Baltimore since 1953, winning back-to-back NFL championships in 1958 and '59 and Super Bowl V in 1970. The fan base was loyal and passionate . . . which is what made the team's sudden departure all the more painful.

Under the cover of darkness on March 28, 1984, Colts owner Robert Irsay (seen here in a shouting match with a reporter) had the moving trucks load up everything that wasn't bolted to the floor and head out to the team's new home, Indianapolis.

Irsay had been fighting with the city of Baltimore for years, trying to get a new stadium deal. There had been rumors of relocation to Indianapolis or Phoenix, but nothing was imminent. Indianapolis was also hoping to get an expansion franchise, but when the NFL

announced in January 1984 that expansion was being put on hold, the city stepped up talks with Irsay.

To counter, Baltimore city officials discussed a plan to seize ownership of the Colts by eminent domain. This infuriated Irsay, and he immediately made the decision to move.

Stunned Colts fans were heartbroken. Hall of Fame quarterback Johnny Unitas, who stayed in Baltimore after his playing days, cut off all ties with the team. The Baltimore Colts Marching Band did not go to Indianapolis. The band was told about the secret move the night before it happened, so they were able to get their instruments out of the office before the moving trucks started packing. They continued to perform in parades and at football halftimes . . . but never in Indianapolis.

74

REGGIE WHITE SIGNS WITH PACKERS

APRIL 6, 1993

In the early days of NFL free agency, Philadelphia Eagles All-Pro defensive end Reggie White was the big fish. He was courted by big-market powers of the day such as the Washington Redskins and San Francisco 49ers, but he shocked the football world when he signed a four-year, $17-million deal with the Packers, a small-market team that hadn't been to the playoffs in 11 years.

"White is the greatest free-agent acquisition since unlimited free agency began in 1993," said NFL historian Elliot Harrison. "He was a godsend for the Packers, in the sense that they badly needed a pass rusher and defensive leadership."

One year earlier, Packers general manager Ron Wolf had orchestrated a trade with the Atlanta Falcons for quarterback Brett Favre. With Favre taking over the offense and now White adding his clout to the defense, Green Bay became a perennial playoff team. They reached their peak in 1996, when the Packers defeated the Patriots in Super Bowl XXXI.

75

EMMITT IS NEW RUSHING KING

OCTOBER 27, 2002

As a 21-year-old rookie with the Dallas Cowboys in 1990, Emmitt Smith rushed for 937 yards. It would be the last time in that century that Smith failed to top 1,000 yards.

In fact, Smith went 11 straight seasons with at least 1,000 yards, an NFL record, including a five-year stretch (1991–95) in which he averaged 1,604 yards per season.

Of course, Smith's success coincided with the return to prominence of "America's Team." Between 1992 and '95, the Cowboys won three Super Bowls. Dallas also had Troy Aikman at quarterback, Michael Irvin at receiver, a world-class offensive line, and the fastest defense in football. To be sure, the Cowboys' success was a team effort, but make no mistake: the team fed off the will and determination of Smith.

A prime example was the final game of the 1993 regular season. Dallas needed to beat the New York Giants on the road in order to clinch the NFC East and earn a playoff bye. The chances of that happening appeared slim when Smith suffered a separated shoulder early in the second quarter. Amazingly, Smith only missed two snaps. And in a defensive struggle, he carried the Cowboys—on one shoulder—to an overtime victory. He carried the ball 32 times for 168 yards, adding 10 receptions for another 61 yards—accounting for 229 of the team's 339 total yards.

Five weeks later, Smith was the MVP of Super Bowl XXVIII, rushing for 132 yards and two touchdowns against the Buffalo Bills.

Smith's streak of 1,000-yard seasons ended in 2002, but that season produced a much greater milestone. In a Week 8 home game against the Seattle Seahawks, Smith passed Walter Payton's career total of 16,726 yards to become the NFL's all-time leading rusher.

Smith signed with the Arizona Cardinals in 2003 and played two more seasons. He retired with 18,355 yards. In addition to the all-time rushing crown, Smith is No. 2 on the all-time list in yards from scrimmage (21,579), and total touchdowns (175).

76

NFL APPROVES NAMES ON JERSEYS

MARCH 18, 1970

When the American Football League officially merged with and became a part of the NFL, several of its groundbreaking innovations were put on hold. The two-point conversion, for instance, which was a staple of the AFL, went away and did not appear in the NFL until 1994. One very important innovation that was adopted after the merger: the 1970 season was the first in which NFL players had their names on the back of their jerseys.

The AFL adopted that policy from the start for a few reasons. For starters, it helped promote the players and provide a little publicity.

In addition, it was a big plus for television viewers, whose numbers were growing exponentially in the '60s.

Some at the NFL were reluctant to approve of the policy, not wanting to give the AFL its due for such a smart move. Fifty years later, it's hard to imagine watching an NFL game without names on the back of jerseys.

It's also hard to imagine how much less money the NFL would earn without this development. The league makes millions each year on jersey sales.

77 BREES BREAKS PASSING RECORD

OCTOBER 8, 2018

When the 2018 NFL regular-season schedule was released, Drew Brees knew exactly what the league was thinking. Week 5. New Orleans Saints home game on Monday night. "Okay, I see what the NFL is doing," Brees thought to himself. "They're anticipating something newsworthy and prime-time worthy. No pressure, right?"

The NFL was spot on. Brees entered the 2018 season needing 1,496 yards to pass Peyton Manning and become the NFL's all-time passing yards leader. All Brees had to do was put up average Brees-like numbers through the first month of the season and he'd be in position to break the record in that Monday night game. And that's exactly what happened.

Brees entered the game against Washington needing 201 yards to break the record. It was inconceivable that he wouldn't do it, but what really made it memorable was the dramatic fashion in which it unfolded.

The play that broke the record was a 62-yard touchdown to rookie receiver Tre'Quan Smith.

"The way that it happened, I don't think you could have drawn it up any better," Brees told ESPN later that night.

After the touchdown, the game was temporarily stopped as the ball was given to Pro Football Hall of Fame officials who were on hand and the home crowd gave Brees a prolonged standing ovation. Brees celebrated with his teammates, and then went to the sideline to create another memorable moment with his family.

"I love you guys so much," Brees said while hugging his three sons. "You can accomplish anything in life if you're willing to work for it."

It was just part of a milestone-filled season for Brees. Two weeks earlier, he had broken Brett Favre's all-time record for completions. A few weeks later, he moved into second place in career TD passes with 520.

78 SUPER BOWL XIII: THE REMATCH

JANUARY 21, 1979

There was plenty of hype leading up to Super Bowl XIII, and for good reason. The Pittsburgh Steelers and Dallas Cowboys were the dominant teams of the decade. Both teams had a pair of Super Bowl victories to their credit, so the winner of this game would be the NFL's first three-time Super Bowl champ.

In addition to Hall of Fame head coaches Chuck Noll and Tom Landry, the game featured a total of 14 future Hall of Fame players (nine for Pittsburgh, five for Dallas).

The game lived up to the hype, too. It was the highest-scoring Super Bowl to that point and it went down to the wire—which was surprising considering the Steelers had built a 35–17 lead with less than seven minutes left in the game. Roger Staubach threw his second touchdown pass of the game to make it 35–24 with 2:27 left. Dallas then recovered an onside kick and Staubach led another scoring drive, throwing his third TD pass with 22 seconds left. This time, Pittsburgh recovered the onside kick and ran out the clock.

With a 35–31 victory, Pittsburgh won the third of its four Super Bowl titles in the '70s. But it might not have happened that way if not for one of the most unfortunate moments in Super Bowl history. Trailing 21–14 late in the third quarter, Dallas drove to the Steelers' 10-yard line. On third down, Staubach found tight end Jackie Smith wide open in the end zone . . . but Smith dropped the pass. A touchdown would have tied the game at 21. Instead, Dallas settled for a field goal and trailed by four—ultimately the difference in the game.

Smith had retired from the St. Louis Cardinals in 1977 after a stellar 15-year career. The Cowboys coaxed him out of retirement in '78 due to injuries at the position. Smith was inducted into the Pro Football Hall of Fame in 1994, but to many he is known more for his Super Bowl drop.

Pittsburgh's Terry Bradshaw, who passed for 318 yards and four touchdowns, won the first of his two Super Bowl MVPs. Lynn Swann caught seven passes for 124 yards and a touchdown. John Stallworth caught three passes for 115 yards and two scores, including a 75-yarder that tied the game at 14 just after Dallas took its only lead of the game early in the second quarter.

"Super Bowl XIII, in my mind, was one of the most memorable Super Bowls," former Cowboys personnel director Gil Brandt told NFL.com. "Those were two great football teams. . . . Even though we lost, I would say Super Bowl XIII was among the greatest Super Bowls."

JANUARY 8, 2000

Buffalo kicker Steve Christie booted a field goal with 16 seconds left to give the Bills a 16–15 lead in an AFC playoff game against the Tennessee Titans. Then the fun began . . .

The Titans, under head coach Jeff Fisher, had this kickoff return in their playbook and practiced it regularly. The play was called "Home Run Throwback," which called for a pair of laterals.

Tennessee's Lorenzo Neal fielded the ensuing kickoff near the right hashmark at the 25-yard line. He quickly handed the ball off to tight end Frank Wycheck, who took a few steps to his right and then chucked the ball across the field to wide receiver Kevin Dyson.

Tyson had actually never practiced "Home Run Throwback"—he was filling in for injured return specialist Derrick Mason and, in fact, he had never returned a kickoff in the NFL. But the play worked to perfection—Dyson raced down the sideline 75 yards to score the stunning, game-winning touchdown.

Four weeks later, the Titans made their first and only Super Bowl appearance, losing to the St. Louis Rams when Dyson was tackled at the 1-yard line on the game's final play trying to score what would have been a game-tying touchdown.

80

ADOPTION OF ROONEY RULE

2003

Pro Football Hall of Famer Fritz Pollard became the NFL's first African American head coach when he took over the Akron Pros, all the way back in 1921. **But there wasn't another African American head coach in the league until the Oakland Raiders hired Art Shell in 1989.**

Not only were opportunities for minority coaches harder to come by, but the pressure to succeed was unfairly magnified. After the 2002 season, highly successful African American coaches Tony Dungy and Dennis Green were both fired. Dungy had a winning record in his six seasons with the Buccaneers; Green was coming off a losing season—but it was his only losing season in 10 years with the Vikings.

The league knew something had to be done. Pittsburgh Steelers owner Dan Rooney, chairman of the NFL's diversity committee, spearheaded the new policy that would come to bear his name.

The Rooney Rule mandated that at least one minority candidate had to be interviewed for any coaching vacancy. The rule was expanded in 2007 to include general manager openings.

Some observers argued that the Rooney Rule put undue pressure on teams that might already have a specific candidate in mind for the job. Proponents of the Rooney Rule argued that the policy did not prevent a team from hiring anyone they wanted. Its purpose was to at least provide a minority coach the opportunity to interview and get noticed.

Speaking at a Fritz Pollard Alliance function in 2014, former NFL commissioner Paul Tagliabue called the Rooney Rule "a commitment to meritocracy, a commitment to intelligence."

Ironically, Rooney's Steelers became a direct beneficiary of the rule.

When the Steelers had to replace Bill Cowher as head coach in 2007, Rooney observed the Rooney Rule by interviewing the Vikings' 34-year-old defensive coordinator Mike Tomlin. Rooney didn't know what to expect, but Tomlin floored him and he got the job. Two years later, Rooney and Tomlin celebrated a victory in Super Bowl XLIII.

"Mike Tomlin wouldn't have gotten this opportunity without this rule," Shell said when Tomlin was first hired. "He never would have sat down with Dan Rooney."

81

BIRTH OF NFL NETWORK

NOVEMBER 4, 2003

The National Football League wasn't the only professional sports entity to come to the realization in the early 2000s that it could be highly advantageous to control its own content. The NFL, NBA, NHL, and Major League Baseball have all launched their own networks. But with a vast archive of NFL Films footage at its disposal, the NFL might have had a leg up in terms of programming.

"I expected it to be an integral part of the viewing experience for the NFL," says NFL Network's Rich Eisen (seen here running his annual 40 at the Combine). "I just didn't know how long it would take."

When did Eisen realize it was going to work? Just 11 weeks in, when the NFL Network was covering its first Super Bowl.

"When we were there, Steve Bornstein and the NFL arranged it so that every few feet in the convention center and radio row, there was a television screen tuned into the NFL Network. You went into the media buses, there was the NFL Network. Every single hotel that anyone was staying at in Houston had a special showing of the NFL Network. And it gave us an idea of what we would look like the day that we would be fully distributed as a true bona fide, everybody-sees-us entity."

Over the years, NFL Network has grown to the point where it airs live regular-season and playoff games as well as the NFL Draft. The network's end-to-end coverage of the annual NFL Combine has made that event appointment viewing for die-hard fans.

82

SUPER BOWL XLIII: THE CATCH

FEBRUARY 1, 2009

A Super Bowl can be legendary if there's one amazing play to look back on—think "Helmet Catch." In Super Bowl XLIII, there were multiple "Oh, wow!" moments.

The most improbable play came late in the second quarter. The Pittsburgh Steelers held a 10–7 lead but the Arizona Cardinals were driving for a go-ahead score. At the 1-yard line, it looked as if Arizona would hit paydirt and take a 14–10 lead into halftime.

With 18 seconds left, Cardinals quarterback Kurt Warner tried to hit Anquan Boldin on a quick slant, but it was intercepted at the goal line by linebacker James Harrison. As the clock wound down to zero, Harrison made a frantic, unbelievable rumble down the right sideline. The 240-pounder came close to stepping out of bounds a few times, but he inexplicably made it 100 yards and into the end zone. It was a potential 14-point swing, and it gave Pittsburgh a 17–7 halftime lead.

"Those last couple of yards was probably tougher than anything I've gone through in my life," Harrison said after the game.

But the Cardinals, playing in their first Super Bowl, came back in the second half. Kurt Warner, who passed for 414 yards for the Rams in Super Bowl XXXIV, threw for another 377 yards and three touchdown passes here. Superstar receiver Larry Fitzgerald, who had been contained in the first half, could not be stopped after halftime. With less than three minutes left to play, Fitzgerald took a short pass up the middle from Warner and went into another gear, splitting defenders and racing 64 yards for his second touchdown of the second half—giving Arizona its first lead of the game at 23–20.

Pittsburgh, playing in its second Super Bowl in four years, started its final drive on its own 22-yard line. A holding penalty put them back on the 12, but then quarterback Ben Roethlisberger calmly marched them down the field. His fourth completion of the drive was a mid-range pass to receiver Santonio Holmes that Holmes broke for 40 yards, setting up the Steelers at the Arizona 6-yard line. Two plays later, Roethlisberger lofted a pass toward Holmes in the corner of the end zone, and Holmes made an amazing, outstretched grab while keeping his toes inbounds.

Holmes, who finished with nine catches for 131 yards and that game-winning score, was the MVP of Pittsburgh's sixth Super Bowl victory.

83 DIRECTV LAUNCHES NFL SUNDAY TICKET

SEPTEMBER 4, 1994

Satellite service DirecTV launched in June of 1994, and it wasn't long after that when they announced a groundbreaking deal with the National Football League.

Prior to the launch of DirecTV's Sunday Ticket package, fans across the country had limited viewing options when it came to Sunday NFL games. The networks broadcasting the games set up regional broadcasts. If you were a Seattle Seahawks fan living in Chicago, the only way you could watch a Seahawks game was if they were playing the Bears or were chosen to be featured in the one national game of the day or on Monday night.

Subscribing to DirecTV changed that forever, giving fans access to all out-of-market games.

Actually, some sports bars were able to tap into satellite services to show out-of-market NFL games two years before Sunday Ticket was created. Believe it or not, that concept was pioneered by entrepreneur and star of the TV show *Bar Rescue*, Jon Taffer.

Taffer was then brought on as a board member of NFL Enterprises, and Sunday Ticket was soon born.

In addition to being a big selling point for DirecTV, it injected new life into the sports bar industry. More and more bars, with a Sunday Ticket subscription, could have multiple games on at the same time. It made sports bars a popular destination every Sunday during the football season.

Deion Sanders, Peyton Manning, and Eli Manning showed off their comedy chops in a series of famous NFL Sunday Ticket commercials.

ON MONDAY, SEPTEMBER 25, 2006, STEVE GLEASON WA
MOST DRAMATIC MOMENTS IN NEW ORLEANS SAINTS HIS
FIRST QUARTER OF THE TEAM'S RETURN TO THE SUPERDO
THAT NIGHT, THE SAINTS DEFEATED THEIR RIVAL ATLANTA FA
AN IMPROBABLE RUN FOR A TEAM THAT WOULD GO ON T
PLAY FOR THE NFC CHAMPIONSHIP THAT SEASON. TH
SYMBOLIZED THE "REBIRTH" OF THE CITY

SCULPTOR, BRIAN P. HANLON
HANLON SCULPTURE STUDIO
2012

84

SAINTS RETURN TO NEW ORLEANS . . . AND STAY THERE

SEPTEMBER 25, 2006

After Hurricane Katrina devastated the city of New Orleans in 2005, one of immediate effects was that the Saints could not play their home games in the Louisiana Superdome. Not only was the stadium too damaged from the storm to host a game, the stadium was also used to house displaced victims of Katrina.

The Saints split their home schedule between LSU's Tiger Stadium in Baton Rouge and the Alamodome in San Antonio. While the team was playing in San Antonio, that city's power brokers were making a strong play to bring the Saints to San Antonio permanently. Owner Tom Benson was having lease issues with New Orleans even before Katrina.

During the 2005 season, NFL commissioner Paul Tagliabue began a series of meetings with Benson and Louisiana governor Kathleen Blanco to find a way to keep the Saints in New Orleans. It was something that meant a lot to Tagliabue.

On September 25, 2006, the Saints played their first regular-season game in the Superdome since Katrina, and it was an emotional victory. Steve Gleason sparked the win with a blocked punt in the first quarter, a moment that has been memorialized with a statue outside the Superdome.

By 2009, a deal was worked out to keep the Saints in the Superdome until at least 2025.

"The NFL's owners went above and beyond to require the Saints to come back to New Orleans," said Tagliabue. "For me, that was the most significant commitment the NFL had ever made to a single community. It was not just a commitment to keep a team in a city but a commitment to keep a city alive. The city was going to die if the NFL had left. The fact that the league made them stay was the most significant thing. Not just for football."

E FOR ONE OF THE
CKED A PUNT IN THE
HURRICANE KATRINA.
IT WOULD KICK—START
SOUTH CROWN AND
NT. THAT SEASON.
ANS.

85

FAVRE HONORS DAD

DECEMBER 22, 2003

Hall of Fame quarterback Brett Favre was a down-home country boy from tiny Kiln, Mississippi. His father, "Big Irv," was his high school coach, and the two were always close. So Favre was understandably devastated when Irvin Favre suffered a massive heart attack and died on Sunday, December 21, 2003. He was 58.

When Brett Favre learned of his father's death, he was with his Packers teammates in a northern California hotel. Green Bay was preparing to face the Oakland Raiders on *Monday Night Football*, the final game of Week 16. It was a huge game for the Packers, who needed a win to remain tied for first with the Minnesota Vikings in the NFC North. Nevertheless, head coach Mike Sherman didn't hesitate in telling Favre not to worry about the game and do what he needs to do for his family.

Favre didn't hesitate, either. He knew Big Irv would want him to play, and his family agreed. Favre announced that he would play in Oakland on Monday night then join his family in Mississippi on Tuesday.

And play he did. Making his 205th consecutive start, then an NFL record for quarterbacks, Favre's tribute to his dad turned into the game of his life. Favre passed for 311 yards and four touchdowns . . . by halftime.

For the game, Favre completed 22 of 30 passes for 399 yards and four touchdowns. His passer rating of 154.9 was a career high.

In a career that featured no shortage of big games, the night Favre played with a heavy heart was his best game.

86

PEYTON RIDES INTO SUNSET

FEBRUARY 7, 2016

The game itself wasn't so special, but the Denver Broncos' 24–10 win over the Carolina Panthers in Super Bowl 50 marked the final game in the legendary career of Peyton Manning.

It's ironic, because two years earlier he had set single-season NFL records with 5,477 yards and 55 touchdowns, only to get crushed in Super Bowl XLVIII by the Seattle Seahawks. In 2015, however, Manning had perhaps his worst season ever. It was revealed after Week 9 that he had a left foot injury, and Brock Osweiler would be filling in for him. Osweiler didn't blow anyone away, but he held his own. Even as Manning was getting healthy, some fans actually wondered who should start in the playoffs.

But when Osweiler struggled early in the regular-season finale, Manning made his return to the lineup, and he then started in playoff wins over the Steelers and then the defending Super Bowl champion Patriots in the AFC title game.

In Super Bowl 50, it was Denver's defense that ruled the day. Manning's final numbers couldn't have been more pedestrian: 13 of 23, 141 yards, no touchdowns, and one interception. But Manning left Levi's Stadium that night with the second Super Bowl crown of his legendary career.

One month later, he announced his retirement after 18 record-breaking seasons.

87

BILL BELICHICK NAMED PATRIOTS HEAD COACH

JANUARY 27, 2000

As defensive coordinator of the New York Giants, he led defenses that stymied two Hall of Fame quarterbacks—first John Elway and then Jim Kelly—in Super Bowl victories. During his five-year stint as head coach of the Cleveland Browns, he led the Browns to their only playoff win in the last 29 years. He was already one of the most respected coaches in the NFL before he became head coach of the New England Patriots, but it was his final coaching destination that made him a legend.

Before he started winning Super Bowls in New England, however, there was the bizarre set of circumstances that culminated in his hiring. Belichick was the New York Jets defensive coordinator under Bill Parcells when New England fired Pete Carroll after the 1999 season. Patriots owner Robert Kraft made it known he wanted to hire Belichick. Parcells, who had a rocky relationship with Kraft after his days as Patriots coach, quickly announced that he was stepping down as Jets head coach, remaining with the team in a front-office capacity, and naming Belichick his successor.

The next day, Belichick was introduced to the local media as new Jets head coach . . . and it was there he announced he was resigning.

With the Jets about to be sold after the death of former owner Leon Hess, Belichick explained that he was concerned about the potential new owners. Whatever the reason, Kraft quickly stepped in and hired Belichick. The Jets argued that Belichick was still under contract, and NFL commissioner Paul Tagliabue ruled that New England had to give the Jets a first-round draft pick as compensation.

It's safe to say the compensation was worth it. Belichick went 5–11 in his first season in New England and he hasn't had a losing season since. He's taken the Patriots to nine Super Bowls and won it six times—more NFL championships than any other coach in league history.

Belichick was 67 years old when the 2019 season began. It's doubtful he'll stick around long enough to pass record-holder Don Shula, but he entered 2019 third on the all-time list for coaching victories, 32 behind George Halas for second place.

GOODELL NAMED COMMISSIONER

AUGUST 8, 2006

Any parents trying to convince their children about the importance of internships need only present one example: Roger Goodell. After college in 1981, Goodell wrote letters to the NFL office and to every NFL team inquiring about work. In 1982, he secured a role as an administrative intern at the league office. In 1983, he became an intern with the New York Jets. A year later, the NFL hired him as an assistant in the public relations department. From there, Goodell worked his way up to COO under commissioner Paul Tagliabue and, ultimately, Tagliabue's successor.

While Goodell has had his fair share of public criticism, he has also presided over the NFL's major growth in the areas of business, technology, and media.

"Roger Goodell as commissioner has taken advantage of new technology to present NFL football on an ever-changing variety of platforms and has brought the games and our ancillary programming to a wider audience of fans," said longtime NFL executive Joe Browne. "He also was at the forefront in labor negotiations, which resulted in a 10-year labor agreement in 2011 that brought stability for the players, owners, and NFL fans."

Goodell's background as a businessman has helped to elevate the NFL into a year-round, event-driven organization. His tenure has seen the rise of fantasy football, the move to hold the annual NFL Draft in different venues around the country, and the improved program offerings on NFL Network.

"Roger has said on several occasions that as a young NFL employee he was fortunate to work for the two finest commissioners ever in sports—Pete Rozelle and Paul Tagliabue," said Browne. "One day, 21st century NFL employees proudly will include Roger in that elite group."

89 NFL ADOPTS INSTANT REPLAY

MARCH 11, 1986

When it comes to tech advancements or experimental ideas that could be controversial, the NFL usually prefers to play it conservative and let other leagues dip their toes in the water before diving in. For that reason, it's notable that the NFL actually led the way when it came to the use of instant replay.

NFL execs began researching and toying with instant replay as far back as the mid-1970s, but it wasn't until the 1985 preseason that it started being used. That experiment worked so well that owners approved limited use of replay for the 1986 regular season and playoffs. The vote was 23–4–1 (it needed 21 votes to pass).

Replays were reviewed from an in-stadium booth and then relayed down to the officials on the field. There were no coach's challenges at this point, and reviewable plays were limited to issues of possession or illegal touching; plays on the sidelines, goal line, or end lines; and "easily detectable infractions" (like too many men on the field).

Owners were cautious enough about instant replay—their main concern being the potential to make games longer—that they only approved it on the condition that it come up for vote again at the end of each season.

"I'm confident the system will get better and better," Hall of Fame Miami Dolphins coach Don Shula said after the '87 vote. "As coaches, we realized we can't see a game from the sidelines as well as our coaches can from upstairs in the press box. If you transmit that same thinking to officials, it helps them too."

In 1991, however, owners reversed their vote and replay was done after six years. There was no instant replay from 1992 to '98, with the exception of some experimentation in 1996 preseason games.

After more tweaking to the procedure, owners approved replay for the '99 season, and it's been in place ever since.

Dick "Night Train" Lane intercepts a pass against the Packers in a December 1952 game in Los Angeles, California.

90

FOX LANDS NFL RIGHTS

DECEMBER 17, 1993

In the early '90s, the television world was ruled by the three major broadcast networks, and all three of them had a significant NFL package of their own. CBS had the NFC games, NBC had AFC games, and ABC had *Monday Night Football*. These packages were up after the 1993 season, and NFL commissioner Paul Tagliabue was looking to broker lucrative new deals.

Tagliabue understood that the best way to bring up the price tag was to have more competition. He had recently added a Sunday night package that was shared by cable networks ESPN and Turner. In order to stir the pot for the bigger packages, Tagliabue and some league owners—notably Jerry Jones of the Cowboys—began talking to upstart broadcast network Fox.

Fox had launched in 1986, and it had some popular programs like *The Simpsons* and *The X-Files*, but it struggled to compete with the big three networks. Fox executives recognized that having an NFL package could instantly boost its viewership and its credibility, so they went all in. The NFC was considered the most appealing of the packages, as it had the bigger markets and the most popular teams. Fox knew they had to make the NFL an offer they couldn't refuse—and that's exactly what happened.

Fox landed the NFC package with an offer of $1.58 billion over four years—reportedly $400 million more than CBS had bid. As they began to build their football presence, Fox continued to make a splash by hiring some of CBS' top talent—John Madden and Pat Summerall to call games and Terry Bradshaw for its pregame show.

Flashing the slogan "Same Game, New Attitude," Fox had an immediate impact on the NFL on TV.

"If you look at the coverage and what people do in sports now, it looks more like what we did than it did before we were there," veteran TV executive Tracy Dolgin told The Ringer in 2018. "It's gone our way. . . . The kinds of things you see now are very different than if Fox had not come in and said, 'It's okay to treat sports as entertainment.'"

91 MICHAEL STRAHAN BREAKS SACK RECORD, WITH HELP

JANUARY 6, 2002

Before he won a Super Bowl and before he became a TV star, Michael Strahan was a menace to opposing quarterbacks from his perch as defensive end for the New York Giants.

Strahan finished his 15-year career with 141.5 sacks, sixth on the all-time list. He had six seasons with at least 11 sacks, including an NFL-record 22.5 sacks in 2001.

Strahan was particularly unstoppable that year. He was held without a sack in the Giants' first two games of the season, but then they started coming in bunches.

He had three against the Saints in Week 3 and four against the Rams in Week 5. After getting 3.5 sacks of Donovan McNabb in a Week 16 game against the Eagles, Strahan was sitting at 21.5 sacks with one game left in the season.

Mark Gastineau's 17-year-old NFL record was 22.

With less than three minutes to play in the regular-season finale against Green Bay, Strahan was still at 21.5. The Packers had the football and were nursing a comfortable lead. Packers head coach Mike Sherman sent in a running play, but quarterback Brett Favre called an audible. Favre—a good friend of Strahan's—faked the handoff and rolled out to his left, Strahan's side.

Because the offensive linemen thought it was a running play, they weren't in pass protection mode. Strahan had a free path to Favre, who gave himself up and let Strahan fall on him for the record-breaking sack.

Favre denied that he gave his friend a gift, but few believed him.

"Strahan can get sacks on his own," Sherman said after the game. "We don't have to give it to him."

Downtime in a 1923 game at Bellevue Park in Green Bay where
the Chicago Bears beat the Packers by a score of 3–0.

92 APFA BECOMES NFL; DECATUR STALEYS BECOME CHICAGO BEARS

JUNE 24, 1922

What's in a name? In this case, a lot. Two years after the American Professional Football Association was formed, it officially changed its name to the National Football League. At the time, there were no teams west of Chicago or south of Washington, D.C., so "national" might not have been the most appropriate descriptor. Marketing may not have gone into the decision, but think of the ramifications of the name change. Would fans have embraced the "APFA" as easily as they did the "NFL?" NFL just sounds better, doesn't it?

At the same time as that name change, one of the league's original teams also made a move. Actually, the Decatur Staleys moved 180 miles north to Chicago in 1921. The Chicago Staleys won the NFL title that season. A year later, team owner George Halas renamed the team the Chicago Bears.

Again, not really a marketing decision, but it worked out pretty well. Would that *Saturday Night Live* bit have been as good if it was "Da Staleys?"

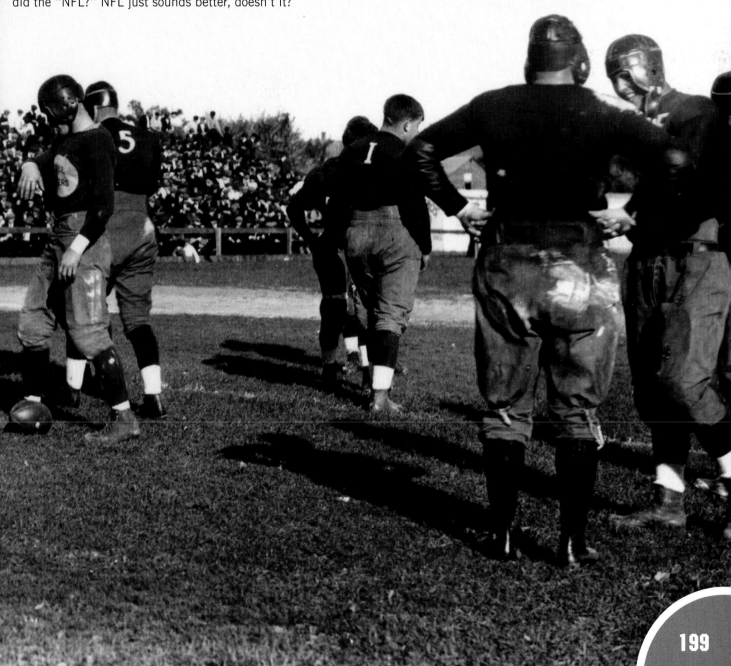

93

RAMS-COLTS FRANCHISE TRADE

JULY 13, 1972

Most NFL insiders will tell you that the biggest block-buster trade in NFL history was the 1989 deal that sent running back Herschel Walker from the Dallas Cowboys to the Minnesota Vikings. In exchange for Walker and three draft picks, the Cowboys got a combination of 13 players and picks. Dallas head coach Jimmy Johnson used that windfall of picks to rebuild a team that would soon win three Super Bowls.

Sure, that was a big trade. But it pales in comparison with the blockbuster deal that took place on July 13, 1972. How can any trade be bigger than one in which both teams essentially got a new owner?

That's exactly what happened when Robert Irsay bought the Los Angeles Rams . . . and then traded the franchise to Carroll Rosenbloom in exchange for the Baltimore Colts. Players and coaches were unaffected. They all remained with their previous team.

Rosenbloom (right) had been a majority owner of the Colts since 1953 and became principal owner in 1964. But eight years later, he was looking for a way out. He was unhappy with the team's stadium deal, disappointed in the fans, and feuding with media. When Irsay, who was a big fan of legendary Colts quarterback Johnny Unitas (left), was looking into buying the Rams, Rosenbloom saw his way out.

Trading franchises was the perfect solution for Rosenbloom. Because a straight exchange of property is not subject to taxes, Rosenbloom saved himself an estimated $4.4 million in capital gains tax.

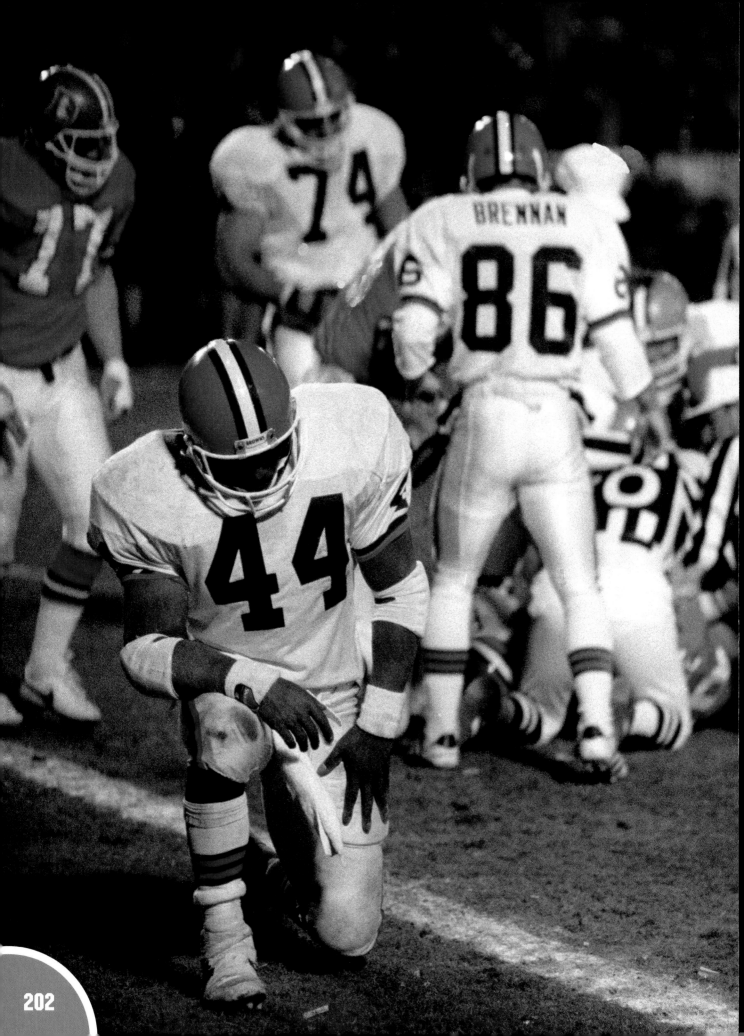

94

THE FUMBLE

JANUARY 7, 1988

One year after John Elway orchestrated "The Drive" to beat Cleveland in the 1986 AFC Championship Game, the two teams met again in the 1987 AFC title game.

Would this finally be Cleveland's year? The Browns' playoff win over the Jets in the '86 postseason had been their first playoff victory since the merger in 1970. They bounced back from the heartbreaking loss to Denver in the '86 AFC title game by winning their third straight AFC Central crown with a 10–5 record, then dispatched the Colts, 38–21, in the divisional round.

The host Broncos jumped out to a 21–3 lead in the AFC title game, but Cleveland stormed back in the second half on the heels of quarterback Bernie Kosar's three touchdown passes. Midway through the fourth quarter, the game was tied at 31. Elway threw a 20-yard touchdown to Sammy Winder to give Denver a 38–31 lead with six minutes left. Still, the Browns weren't ready to throw in the towel.

They got the ball one last time, starting a drive with 3:53 left from their own 25-yard line. It wasn't as dramatic as Elway's performance a year earlier, but Kosar moved his team downfield, with running back Earnest Byner gaining chunks of yards as both a runner and receiver. Cleveland got to Denver's 8-yard line, where they faced a first-and-5 with 1:12 left to play.

Byner got another handoff and he looked like he was going to score his third touchdown of the game to force overtime. But Denver defensive back Jeremiah Castille stripped him of the ball at the 3-yard line. The Broncos recovered the fumble and went to their second straight Super Bowl.

After back-to-back seasons coming so close to the Super Bowl, the Browns haven't been to the AFC Championship Game since.

95

ROGER STAUBACH AND THE NFL'S FIRST HAIL MARY

DECEMBER 28, 1975

The term "Hail Mary" as it pertains to last-second desperation plays in football goes back almost 100 years, though it was not commonplace and it typically was relegated to Catholic schools like Notre Dame. It didn't start to seep into mainstream sports vernacular until this play that helped the Dallas Cowboys stun the Minnesota Vikings in the 1975 NFC divisional playoffs.

Trailing 14–10 in the waning seconds of the game in Minnesota's Metropolitan Stadium, Cowboys quarterback Roger Staubach launched a long pass down the right sideline in the direction of receiver Drew Pearson. Knocked down after the ball left his hands, Staubach didn't know what happened.

"I just threw it and prayed," Staubach said after the game. "I couldn't see whether or not Drew had caught it. I didn't know we had the touchdown until I saw the official raise his arms."

Indeed, Pearson actually had to stop and come back to the ball—some think he pushed off Vikings defender Nate Wright, but it wasn't called. He caught the ball inside the 5-yard line and slipped past Wright into the end zone for the game-winning, 50-yard score.

Staubach referred to the play as a "Hail Mary" in the locker room after the game, and the term became a staple of the sport.

The winning touchdown was miraculous, but there was also some divine intervention on the play just before it. The Cowboys faced a fourth-and-16 from their own 25. Staubach found Pearson on the right sideline—Pearson had to jump for the ball, and a Vikings defender pushed him out of bounds before he came down. Rules at the time gave officials the ability to make the judgment call that if a receiver would have come down in bounds if not for being pushed, it should be ruled a catch. The Vikings argued the call, saying Pearson would not have come down in bounds, but Dallas was awarded the first down at the 50.

Ramifications of the "Hail Mary Game" were significant. The Vikings had been to back-to-back Super Bowls, so the loss ended Minnesota's two-year reign as NFC champions. The Cowboys defeated the Los Angeles Rams in the NFC title game a week later, advancing to Super Bowl X, where they lost to the defending champion Pittsburgh Steelers.

96

JOE CARR NAMED PRESIDENT OF APFA

APRIL 30, 1921

When the American Professional Football Association, soon to be renamed the National Football League, was born in 1920, it named Jim Thorpe as the organization's first president. The reasoning was simple—Thorpe, a player with the Canton Bulldogs, was the most famous person involved in the league, thanks to his days as a college football All-American and an Olympic star.

In 1921, Thorpe was replaced as league president by Joe Carr, who managed the Columbus Panhandles. Carr, seen here giving a watch to Giants captain Mel Hein, had previous experience in professional basketball and minor league baseball, and was the perfect choice to bring stability and growth to the upstart league.

Carr's influence was critical in the early days of the NFL. Among other things, he introduced the standardized player contract and maintained a strong relationship with college football (which was more popular at the time) by implementing and enforcing rules that kept NFL teams from signing players until their college eligibility was complete.

Carr recognized the importance of expanding the league into big markets, playing a key role in bringing a franchise to New York. He also urged coaches to throw more passes, recognizing that the game needed to be more exciting in order to appeal to more fans.

Ben Roethlisberger throws through the snow during a December 2005 game in Pittsburgh.

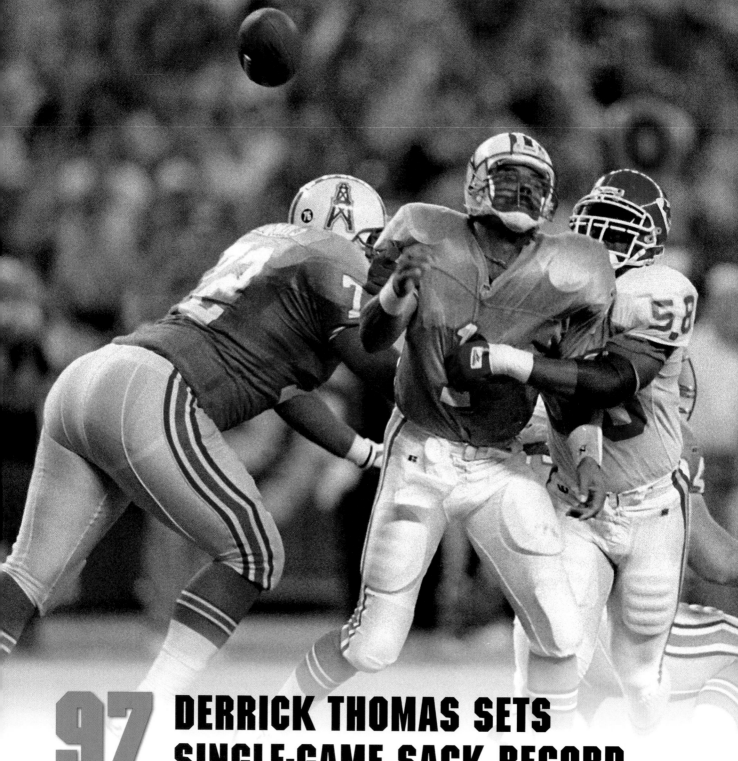

97 DERRICK THOMAS SETS SINGLE-GAME SACK RECORD

NOVEMBER 11, 1990

Few pass rushers in NFL history have been feared quite as much as Kansas City Chiefs outside linebacker Derrick Thomas (seen above practicing his trade). The former Alabama star captured college football's Butkus Award in 1988 when he set an NCAA single-season record with 27 sacks. A few months later, he was the fourth overall pick of the 1989 NFL Draft. He made an immediate impact in the league, notching 10 sacks on the way to becoming the NFL Defensive Rookie of the Year.

There most certainly was no sophomore slump for this dynamic star. Thomas doubled his sack total in 1990—finishing just two sacks shy of what was then the single-season NFL record of 22.

Of those 20 sacks in 1990, seven of them came in one game—still an NFL record. In a Week 10 home game against the Seattle Seahawks, Thomas took quarterback Dave Krieg to the Arrowhead Stadium turf seven times.

Amazingly, he could easily have had eight sacks. The Chiefs led 16–10 but Seattle was driving with time running out. On the last play of the game, Krieg dropped back to pass. Thomas had him wrapped up for sack No. 8, but Krieg somehow wiggled free, scrambled to his left, and fired a game-winning touchdown pass.

"The thing I most remember about that game is the sack I didn't get," Thomas said after the game, "and that's the one that haunts me."

Thomas had 126.5 sacks in his 11 seasons in the NFL, currently 17th on the all-time list. He would rank higher, but his life was tragically cut short on February 8, 2000, when he died from complications following a car accident. He had just turned 33.

98 CLEVELAND LOSES, KEEPS BROWNS

FEBRUARY 9, 1996

If you look at it on paper, it appears the Cleveland Browns moved after the 1995 season and became the Baltimore Ravens. Upon further review, it was a little trickier than that.

Browns owner Art Modell had been dissatisfied for years with Cleveland Stadium revenues. The Browns and Cleveland Indians shared revenues, but when the Indians got their own baseball park, Jacobs Field, the financial impact hit Modell hard. Midway through the 1995 season, he announced that he was moving the team to Baltimore—giving that city an NFL franchise for the first time since the Colts left for Indianapolis in 1984.

The Browns had been a fixture in Cleveland since 1946. With fans in an uproar, the city of Cleveland sued Modell and the Browns, noting that the team's lease stipulated they play their home games in Cleveland Stadium until at least 1998.

With the NFL stepping in, the conflict was resolved. Modell received approval to move his team to Baltimore—however, he relinquished all of the Browns history and intellectual property. The Baltimore team would adopt a new name—thus, the Ravens were born. As part of the deal, it was promised that Cleveland would have a new team in place by 1999. The team would be built from scratch like an expansion team, but it would be called the Cleveland Browns and retain all the history and records of the Browns team that played there from 1946 to 1995.

Roger Staubach and Tony Dorsett of the Dallas Cowboys come out for player introductions just before Super Bowl XIII on January 21, 1979, at the Orange Bowl in Miami, Florida.

99

ADRIAN PETERSON'S SINGLE-GAME RUSHING RECORD

NOVEMBER 4, 2007

Minnesota Vikings running back Adrian Peterson broke the NFL's single-game rushing record when he amassed 296 yards on the ground in a 35–17 win over the San Diego Chargers.

Peterson, a rookie at the time, had 253 yards in the second half alone. But he almost fell short of the record.

With the outcome well in hand, Peterson was taken out of the game with less than two minutes to play and 293 yards. In the press box, a member of the Vikings PR staff realized that Peterson was just two yards shy of the single-game mark that was held by Jamal Lewis. He notified Minnesota's coaching staff and they got Peterson back on the field for the final three yards.

Peterson's record-breaking performance that day was just part of one of the greatest rookie seasons in NFL history. The seventh overall pick in the 2007 NFL Draft, Peterson set personal goals of rushing for 1,300 yards and being named NFL Offensive Rookie of the Year. He accomplished both.

His 296-yard effort was actually his second 200-yard game of the season, making him the first rookie to ever do that. He finished the season with 1,341 rushing yards and 12 touchdowns.

Peterson finished the 2018 season ranked eighth on the all-time rushing list with 13,318 yards.

100

REDZONE CHANNEL LAUNCH

SEPTEMBER 13, 2009

An offshoot of NFL Network, the RedZone was created to air live cut-ins from all of the Sunday games. The idea was to go live to a game whenever a team was inside the opponent's 20-yard line. It was heaven for fantasy football players consumed with getting scoring updates as fast as possible.

In fact, when NFL TV ratings dipped slightly in 2018, many observers speculated that the RedZone Channel was at fault. They pointed to millenials who didn't have the patience to watch an entire game but were consumed by highlights. This theory was disproved a year later when ratings came back up, but the RedZone's popularity was no fluke.

In particular, there is usually a window—when the early Sunday games are winding down—when the RedZone is must-see TV. With as many as 10 games going on at once, there's usually a few that go down to the wire. So when the timing is right, RedZone can go from one game-winning play to the next—sometimes airing them simultaneously on a split screen.

"And for fantasy football it is a must," said NFL Network's Rich Eisen, who also noted that the RedZone's popularity is a big reason why the NFL Network in general was able to become a cable mainstay.

"The fact that the NFL created its own RedZone Channel for the NFL Network helped crack the code for distribution."

ACKNOWLEDGMENTS

First off, I'd like to thank the team at Triumph Books—Jesse Jordan, Josh Williams, Noah Amstadter, Clarissa Young, Tom Bast, Jon Hahn, and everyone else who helped—for publishing this book. And, of course, my publishing *consigliere*, James Buckley Jr., with whom I've been fortunate to know and work for many years.

Coming up with 100 important moments over the first 100 years of the NFL, let alone putting them in some kind of order, proved to be a challenging but incredibly fun mission. I didn't take it lightly, and I was very appreciative to receive input and feedback from some esteemed experts: Howie Schwab, Jason Cole at Fansided, Jarrett Bell at *USA Today*, Pro Football Talk's Charean Williams, former *Washington Post* sports editor George Solomon, retired *Chicago Tribune* NFL writer Don Pierson, and Pro Football Hall of Fame writer Ray Didinger.

I must also thank a group of former colleagues from my days at the National Football League, beginning with commissioner Paul Tagliabue. Truth be told, commissioner Tagliabue wasn't all that comfortable with the idea of ranking important NFL moments, but his keen knowledge and appreciation for NFL history was inspiring. Along with commissioner Tagliabue, these NFL alumni were of particular help to me: Joe Browne, Jim Steeg, Greg Aiello, and Joel Bussert.

PHOTO ATTRIBUTION

Title Page: Michael Zagaris / Getty Images

Foreword: Peter Brouillet / Getty Images

Introduction: First photo—NFL Photos / AP Photo

Second photo—AP Photo / File

1. NFL Photos / AP Images
2. Focus on Sport / Getty Images
3. AP Photo / File
4. David Stluka / AP Images
5. Nate Fine / Getty Images
6. AP Photo / File
7. Al Messerschmidt / AP Images
8. Peter Read Miller / AP Images
9. Pro Football Hall of Fame / AP Images
10. AP Images
11. AP Images
12. Jamie Squire / Getty Images
13. James Flores / Getty Images
14. AP Images
15. Vernon Biever / NFL Photos / AP Images
16. Focus on Sport / Getty Images
17. Tony Tomsic / AP Images
18. AP Images
19. Don Larson / Getty Images
20. Gene Puskar / AP Images
21. Harry Cabluck / AP Images
22. Pro Football Hall of Fame / NFL Photos / AP Images
23. Focus on Sport / Getty Images
24. AP Images
25. Tami Tomsic / Getty Images
26. Bruce Dierdorff / Getty Images
27. Amy Sancetta / AP Images
28. Paul Spinelli / AP Images
29. Vic Stein / Getty Images
30. Pro Football Hall of Fame / AP Images
31. Paul Spinelli / AP Images
32. Vic Stein / Getty Images
33. Joe Robbins / Getty Images
34. Focus on Sport / Getty Images
35. Sylvia Allen / Getty Images
36. Damian Strohmeyer / Getty Images
37. G. Paul Burnett / AP Images
38. Jamie Squire / Allsport / Getty Images
39. Al Messerschmidt / AP Images
40. AP Images
41. Focus on Sport / Getty Images
42. Getty Images
43. **Both images:** Pro Football Hall of Fame / AP Images
44. Tony Tomsic / AP Images
45. Fred Jewell / AP Images
46. Focus on Sport / Getty Images

47. David Goldman / AP Images

48. AP Images

49. Tony Tomsic / AP Images

50. Tony Tomsic / AP Images

Insert Photos following chapter 50: *(1920s Chicago Bears image)* Pro Football Hall of Fame / AP Images, *(Odell Beckham Jr. image)* Julio Cortez / AP Images

51. Vic Stein / Getty Images

52. Michael Zagaris /Getty Images)

53. Tony Tomsic / AP Images

54. Harry Harris / AP Images

55. Robert Riger / Getty Images)

56. John Hickey / AP Images

57. Jamie Squire / Allsport / Getty Images

58. Al Messerschmidt / AP Images

59. Robert Riger / Getty Images

60. Focus on Sport / Getty Images

61. **Both images:** Paul Natkin / Getty Images

62. David Durochik / AP Images

63. AP Images

64. David Gonzales / AP Images

65. Anthony Neste / Getty Images

66. Chris O'Meara / AP Images

67. NFL Photos / AP Images

68. Paul Spinelli / AP Images

69. Michael Zagaris / Getty Images

70. Richard Drew / AP Images

71. Doug Benc / AP Images

72. Al Messerschmidt / AP Images

73. Bill Smith / AP Images

74. John Biever / Icon Sportswire / Getty Images

75. Tim Sharp / AP Images

76. Focus on Sport / Getty Images

77. **Main photo:** Butch Dill / AP Images, **Inset photo:** Bill Feig / AP Images

78. Focus on Sport / Getty Images

79. Allen Kee / Getty Images)

80. Julie Jacobson / AP Images

81. Thomas E. Witte / AP Images

82. Doug Benc / Getty Images)

83. Brian Ach / AP Images for DIRECTV

84. Jonathan Bachman / Getty Images

85. Jed Jacobsohn / Getty Images)

86. David J. Phillip / AP Images

87. Al Messerschmidt / AP Images

88. M. Spencer Green / AP Images

89. Jamie Squire / Getty Images)

90. Ric Feld / AP Images

91. Al Bello / Getty Images

92. Pro Football Hall of Fame / AP Images

93. Robert Riger / Getty Images

94. Ron Heflin / AP Images

95. Vernon Biever / AP Images

96. AP Images

97. **Three photos:** *(Warren Moon)* Rick Bowmer / AP Images, *(John Elway)* G. Newman Lowrance / AP Images, *(Steve Young)* G. Newman Lowrance / AP Images

98. Tom Pidgeon / Allsport / Getty Images

99. Tom Olmscheid / AP Images

100. Justin Edmonds / Getty Images

Insert (Two-Page, Full-Spread) Photo Attributions:

Insert Photo 1: *(Cam Newton)* Brett Carlsen / Getty Images

Insert Photo 2: *(Earl Campbell)* Focus on Sport/Getty Images

Insert Photo 3: *(Randy Moss)* Gary Rothstein / Icon Sport Media / Getty Images)

Insert Photo 4: *(Packers)* Robert Riger / Getty Images

Insert Photo 5: *(Deion Sanders, Jerry Rice)* Focus on Sport / Getty Images)

Insert Photo 6: *(Night Train Lane)* Harold P. Matosian / AP Images

Insert Photo 7: *(Ben Roethlisberger)* Ezra Shaw / Getty Images)

Insert Photo 8: *(Roger Staubach, Tony Dorsett)* Ross Lewis / Getty Images

Insert Photo 9: *(Saquon Barkley)* Rich Graessle / Icon Sportswire / Getty Images

ABOUT THE AUTHOR

CRAIG ELLENPORT is a veteran sportswriter who has covered the NFL for more than 30 years. He has written several books about the NFL for kids and young adults. During his 12 years as senior editor at NFL.com and director of NFL Publishing, he oversaw production of all NFL publications, serving as co-editor for *The Super Bowl: An Official Retrospective*.